SKETCHES FOR AUTOBIOGRAPHY

ARNOLD BENNETT

★

Sketches
for Autobiography

edited by
James Hepburn

London
GEORGE ALLEN & UNWIN
Boston   Sydney

First published in 1979

GEORGE ALLEN & UNWIN LTD
40 Museum Street, London WC1A 1LU

British Library Cataloguing in Publication Data

Bennett, Arnold
   Sketches for autobiography.
   1. Bennett, Arnold – Biography
   2. Authors, English – 20th century – Biography
   I. Title   II. Hepburn, James
   823'.9'12   PR6003.E6Z/   79-40219

   ISBN 0-04-928041-4

PR
6003
.E6
Z37

Typeset in 11 on 12 point Garamond by Bedford Typesetters Ltd
and printed in Great Britain
by W. & J. Mackay Ltd, Chatham

Contents

Introduction

Arnold Bennett said that his life was very romantic, and it was. He was born in the grim industrial Potteries in 1867, and he grew up there, an undistinguished boy of an undistinguished family (save that he was top boy at school), and he left school to enter his father's law office. After a few years he failed his law examinations (twice), and then at age twenty-one he came to London to become a shorthand clerk in a law office. He remained a clerk for several years, and then he became assistant editor and presently editor of a woman's magazine. This progress took him to age thirty-three and the year 1900, and who could describe it as romantic except Arnold Bennett himself, whose theme was the romance of the commonplace? The sketches, articles, and essays reprinted here present some of the romantic aspects of those years, and also of later years. In this Introduction must be recorded instead the more conventional romance of his life – the transformation of the undistinguished young boy and young man into a famous author. In the decade from 1908 to 1918 he was commonly regarded as the great English novelist of the time, and even in the 1920s he was a formidable figure whose account of his religious experience made a banner headline on the front page of the *Evening Standard* and whose novel *Lord Raingo* was advertised across London on large posters with a picture of him ("horribly revolting", he wrote to a friend).

Perhaps the transformation began in the late 1880s with the unpaid journalism that he wrote for the *Staffordshire Knot* for a few months before he went away to London. The *Knot* had a short life, and the short life was in part supported by Bennett's father, but in any event the items of local news and gossip that

ix

the youth wrote seemed to enjoy a popular success. In London the journalism ceased for a while. But he became acquainted with people who thought he had talent, and they presently encouraged him to enter a short story contest in *Tit-Bits*, and he won it, in 1891, and after another four years they encouraged him to write a novel, and he wrote it (*A Man from the North*). It is startling to look at the slender and almost wholly frivolous body of writing of the years 1887 to 1893 and think that this was the beginning for a man who in the next thirty-seven years would produce over a hundred books of several sorts, some of them highly esteemed – novels, short story collections, essay collections, plays, opera libretti, journals, autobiography, literary criticism, travel, and pocket philosophy. Among the novels reckoned in at least certain quarters to be substantial are *Anna of the Five Towns* (1902), *Buried Alive* (1908), *The Old Wives' Tale* (1908), the *Clayhanger* trilogy (1910, 1911, 1916), *The Card* (1911), *The Pretty Lady* (1918), *Riceyman Steps* (1923), *Lord Raingo* (1926), and *Imperial Palace* (1930).

Of course a hundred books are unromantic if a life has been consumed in scribbling them. But in the 1890s and the first years of the new century Bennett discovered the resources of a mind that made his task easy. He wrote to his literary agent in 1904: "You would be under a false impression if you imagined that I am working at pressure. I am not. I could do lots more. I have vast leisure." He wrote *The Grand Babylon Hotel* in one month in 1900; he took eight months to write *The Old Wives' Tale* in 1907–8, and wrote a good many articles at the same time; he wrote the 160,000 words of *Clayhanger* in five months in 1910. In his vast leisure he had a romantic career as a watercolourist, and another romantic career as an amateur pianist. These careers are largely unknown, but something of the former can be glimpsed in "Graphic Art in Paris". Eugene Goossens – for whom he wrote the libretti of two operas in the 1920s – said that among literary men of his acquaintance only Shaw knew more about music. There was also his career as a man of nature who spent many hours, many days, walking in the forest of Fontainebleau, and even more hours and more days sailing along the English and European coasts. The two essays on the forest of Fontainebleau are the most obviously romantic pieces of writing included here, and they may surprise readers who know only the plain common-sensical and worldly Bennett. The love of sailing was a love from youth onward, and in the year 1912 – when his writing earned as much money as he had earned all together in the years beforehand, and when *Milestones* was the great hit in the West End – in that year he bought a yacht, and later in the year he sailed it for a month along the Dutch coast, and two years later he published *From the Log of the "Velsa"*. For he wrote on the yacht; he lived on it as in a home where he wrote novels and kept journals. In 1920 he bought a larger yacht – the yacht that Ezra Pound deplored in *Hugh Selwyn Mauberley* in the same year, for Pound had an unromantic view of Bennett (a view that he later admitted was based at least in part on ignorance).

Bennett was an inveterate traveller to romantic places. In the 1890s he travelled to Belgium and France. When in 1903 he was free from a job that tied him to a place and free of obligations to his parents, he packed his bags and went to Algeria and then to France. Having made his home in London for several years and then on a farm in Bedfordshire for two years, he settled in Paris for a few years and then in the French countryside for another few years. In 1913 he came back to England to make his chief residence in Essex for ten years, and then he returned to London. He travelled on the Continent many times, he visited America in 1911, he sailed in the Mediterranean with Otto Kahn in 1927, he went to Russia with Lord Beaverbrook in 1929. The best of his travel books is *Paris Nights* (1913), which has sections on Paris, London, Italy, the Riviera, Fontainebleau, Switzerland, the English Midlands. Several pieces from it are reprinted here.

H. G. Wells, a long-standing friend, wrote to him once with pardonable flattery, "You have the best mind in Europe (in many respects)." Despite such respects, he never became the intellectual or the esthete or the highbrow. The romance of his life did not entail his becoming superior to the many and intelligible to the few. In the 1920s he wrote for the *Criterion, Life and Letters,* the *Adelphi,* the *London Mercury,* and the *New Statesman* (of which he was a director for many years), and he also wrote for the *Express* papers and the *Sunday Pictorial.* He did not elevate his style for the one group, nor did he condescend to the other. In 1927 his secretary wrote to his literary agent to say that a letter from a miner needed answering: Bennett was away, and perhaps the agent could reply for him. The miner ran an educational course for fellow miners, and he wrote to Bennett frequently for advice and help, and Bennett himself customarily replied. How many famous authors conduct such correspondence? Bennett received and answered similar letters for many years. His earliest large successes were in providing light entertainment for a mass audience and in giving them advice (with *The Grand Babylon Hotel* in 1901–2 and the anonymous "Savoir-Faire Papers" in *T.P.'s Weekly* in 1902–3). He wrote to his literary agent about the "Savoir-Faire Papers": "Anyone who wants to know what sort of effect these things have on a solid regular public of 150,000 a week has only got to enquire at the editorial department of *T.P.'s W.*" His agent thought such writing would damage Bennett's reputation if it was reprinted under his name, and it was not reprinted. Four years later Bennett wrote another series for the *Evening News* and signed his name to it and published it in book form. He said of it years later:

> *How to Live on Twenty-Four Hours a Day* sold very well from the start; it still has a steady sale, and it has brought me more letters of appreciation than all my other books put together. I followed it up with a dozen or more books in a similar vein. And I do not suppose that my reputation would have been any less dreadful than it is if I had never published a line for plain people about the management of daily experience.

The romantic imagination that envisioned the lives of Constance and Sophia Baines and Edwin Clayhanger would not divorce itself from the ordinary reality from which those characters derived. He wrote in his *Journal* in 1896: "Essential characteristic of the really great novelist: a Christ-like, all-embracing compassion." He thought the really great novelist was Dostoevsky, and he said of *Clayhanger* while writing it, "It assuredly isn't within 10 miles of Dostoevsky." His own compassion was more ordinary. Reprinted here are a few articles of advice for plain people. They show his romantic concern for ordinary men, and his extraordinary ability to speak to them because he was ordinary too. No account of his life makes sense that fails to emphasise this quality. He arrived at fame and wealth far beyond the ordinary, and enjoyed them, but the gross image of him depicted by Ezra Pound and repeated by Virginia Woolf in her diaries merely tells against literary snobbism.

II

When Bennett was dying in 1931, Frank Swinnerton wrote an appreciation of him that began, "Arnold Bennett was the best, the kindest, the most generous, and the greatest man with whom I have ever come into close contact." Forty-seven years later, Mr Swinnerton reprinted the appreciation in *Arnold Bennett, A Last Word,* and elsewhere in that book he remarked upon another quality: Bennett's reticence. The two men were intimate friends, but Bennett did not talk about his private life or the state of his soul. He never talked about them to anyone. When he wrote autobiography he wrote about the externals of his life, and he did not write about them at length. He kept a journal for thirty-four years, and it is the record of what an observant man saw about him in the ordinary way of seeing, and insofar as it concerns himself it describes what another observant man would have seen in the ordinary way. Sometimes it is not even that. Thus on 15 June 1906: "At 5 P.M. on this day in the forest of Fontainebleau I became engaged to marry Eleanora." On 3 August 1906: "At 11 A.M. on this day, at Caniel, my engagement to Eleanora was broken off." That is all, at least in the published *Journal.* No out-pourings of joys and hopes and fears and failures, no analyses of characters, motives, and desires, no probings into secret selves, and not even Eleanora's full and correct name (Eleanor Green) or the sort of hat she was wearing or the sort of day it was. When Bennett began his journal in 1896 he vowed (according to his friend George Sturt) that "there were to be no vapourings or rhapsodies; introspection was ruled out; speculation on the riddle of the universe was discountenanced". He kept his word, as he always kept it.

Of course he did write one autobiography of some length, *The Truth About an Author*, in 1903. It was a frank account of a certain aspect of his life, and it embarrassed some people; but again it was frank not about the private man but about the typical author. He told stories on himself in Grub Street that were familiar stories in the lives of other authors on the same street, stories that made the literary life seem less exalted than it ought to be. Not that Bennett lacked a high ideal of literature, but the high ideal itself was expressed in detached, ironic terms: "say another thirty years of these emotional ingenuities, these interminable variations on the theme of beauty", he wrote, thinking of the hundred books still ahead of him and only twenty-eight years in fact. *The Truth About an Author* is a remarkable little book, and several years later Bennett said that it "comprised nearly all that I cared to say concerning myself from my cradle up to about the time when I left England for France"; but it would satisfy no' one's craving for autobiography except Bennett's.

In the opening of "The Greatest Moment" (reprinted here) Bennett remarks that "of course there are sensational moments in life particulars of which only a very communicative man will communicate to the world". He little knew how very communicative a lot of people were presently to become, and his own communication in that article was discreet if amusing. Apparently even under stress – perhaps most especially under stress – he did not yield to any temptation to reveal all. No doubt his stammer would have got in the way of speech, and his pen was always under control. He visited the Western Front in the First World War at the request of the Government, and he was ill afterwards, and his wife and Frank Swinnerton were certain that he was gravely upset by what he saw, imagined, and felt; but no word of his suggests such upset, and his published account of the trip, *Over There* (1915), is a superficial record intended to serve country and cause.

It follows, then, that the present collection is meagre fare in the way of revelation. In fact many of the pieces are not autobiographical in the strict sense of the term, and they are included here only because everything that Bennett wrote was autobiographical in a loose sense. For he had a romantic view of writing, derived from the romantic poets. "The book is nothing but the man trying to talk to you, trying to impart to you some of his feelings", he said in *Literary Taste* in 1909; and again he said in *The Author's Craft* in 1914, "When the real intimate work of creation has to be done – and it has to be done on every page – the novelist can only look within for effective aid." An editor once accused him of caricaturing the Duchess of Sutherland in *The Card*, and he replied, "There is only one portrait to be found in all my books – myself." No one who has really read his Bennett – novels, plays, essays, or anything else – would think otherwise. There is the detached, compassionate and gravely humorous narrator who tells the story of Constance and Sophia Baines, there is the more gaily compassionate and sardonic narrator of the comic novels, there is the harshly sardonic critic of Lloyd George's government in the long series of articles in the *Daily News* during the War. They are each and all of them the man himself, very vividly rendered, present, as he says, on every page.

So this reticent man (and realistic novelist) spent his life talking about himself, presenting himself to the public. What he presented was what you might see if you knew him in the ordinary way: an ordinary man at home or on the street; not a man in a dream or nightmare or crisis, not a man psychologised or analysed. It is merely exaggeration to say that readers of his writing might know him almost as well as Mr Swinnerton knew him. And what readers did know usually inspired confidence. Miners wanting help, girls thinking about suicide, Americans desirous of knowing what happened to Cyril Povey after the end of the novel – they all wrote to him, and not in vain. Surely the anger and annoyance he evoked in some readers reflected equally their awareness of the man in his work.

The selection of material for this collection was therefore difficult. The aim was to include all sketches, articles, and essays that were autobiographical in the strict sense, and to include others that seemed to have an important autobiographical aspect. Several accounts of the Potteries are included that have nothing explicitly to do with Bennett himself; but insofar as the Potteries were his home and occupied his imagination for many years, his description of them is a significant part of his self-portrait. They are rather more extensive than comparable material in the novels, and three of them have the virtue of never having been reprinted after their original appearance in the periodical press. It was decided in the main not to use the *Journal* and *The Truth About an Author*. Excerpting the former would be an impossible task, and excerpting the latter to any large extent would tear the book apart. Nevertheless the *Journal* is represented. Bennett often composed articles out of material in it, sometimes with virtually no change, and did so with "Railway Accident at Mantes"; sometimes he made an almost fictional transformation, as with "Evening with Exiles". *The Truth About an Author* is represented by a brief fragment from one of its most delightful parts. Fourteen of the pieces are reprinted for the first time since their original appearance in periodicals or in the privately printed Christmas book of 1908, *Things Which Have Interested Me*. The pieces have been arranged chronologically by the time in Bennett's life to which they refer rather than chronologically according to composition. This has meant the splitting up of the sequence of four sketches concerned with France that were written as a single work and published as "My Reminiscences". Bennett seems to have begun writing these sketches as a kind of sequel to *The Truth About an Author,* but they are much slighter in size and scope, and not a great deal is lost in fitting them in among other pieces.

One last thing must be said, and that by Bennett. In some unpublished journal notes from 1926 he wrote about himself in an unusual vein. His words confirm and contradict some of the things said here, but more especially they cast the whole of his life into a new light:

I rarely worry in a practical way about happiness or unhappiness. I just enjoy it or stick it. I seldom ask myself what gives me most happiness or unhappiness. It is only on the rare occasions when I deliberately enquire into it that I realise that my most satisfactory time is from early morning to after breakfast, and that nothing gives me a purer pleasure than the first half of a fine cigar. I never worry about a future life; & very rarely even think about it for a moment, or about a God. These things simply have no interest for me whatever. Although I have slowly acquired a scientific habit of thought, I have only applied it to the not-me part of the universe, scarcely ever to the Me. I have been an Instinct more than anything else. I have rarely said I must do so and so in order to obtain so-and-so. I like nothing extremely, except a yacht. I don't really mind where I live and work. I could adjust myself to almost any environment. I am not interested in money. I have not had a clear & fixed ambition. I began to write novels because my friends said that I could. The same for plays. But I always had a feeling for journalism, which feeling is as strong today as ever it was. I scarcely ever analyse my own character . . .

Acknowledgments

Arnold Bennett's essays are reprinted by permission of the Estate of the late Mrs Dorothy Cheston Bennett. Doubleday & Company's permission is also acknowledged for the essays reprinted from *Paris Nights*, *Things that have Interested Me* and *Mental Efficiency*.

The passage from the manuscript "Some Impressions" is used with the kind permission of the Henry W. and Albert A. Berg Collection of the New York Public Library, Astor, Lennox and Tilden Foundations.

The Making of Me

Bennett's ancestry traces back uncertainly to one Anthony Bennett of Burslem who died in 1642. He was a man of no distinction in his small community. He and his wife Elizabeth had eight children, one of whom was baptised in the year 1624. That date provides the earliest known record of the family. Descended from Anthony and Elizabeth in the third generation was Thomas Bennett, born in 1692 and married in 1716 to Hannah Lovatt. Their second daughter, Mary, bore a son out of wedlock in the year 1760. By some report the father was James Brindley (1716–72), the canal engineer. The bastard son John (1760–99) was Bennett's great-great-grandfather. The nearer ancestry on the paternal side included Sampson Bennett (John's son), who was a potter and also at one time keeper of a cheese and bacon stall; in his adult years he turned Wesleyan Methodist. His son John (1813–70) became a Sunday School Superintendent; he was a potter's thrower and also a shopkeeper, and later built Sneyd Pottery. He married Mary Vernon in 1834, and among their six children, three of whom died at an early age, were John Bennett (born 1841), who became a pottery painter, Enoch (born 1843), who became Arnold Bennett's father, and Sarah (died 1924), who married Samuel Barlow, a plumber. Enoch Bennett began life in the pottery trade, and in the middle 1860s he was co-manager of Eagle Pottery in Burslem. The firm failed in 1866, and he then became a draper and pawnbroker in Hope Street, Hanley. Upon the death of his father in 1870 he was able to article himself as a solicitor's clerk. Son Enoch Arnold was born at the drapery-pawnbroking shop on 27 May 1867.

On the maternal side Bennett was descended from the Longsons and Claytons. His maternal grand-father, Robert Longson, married Frances Clayton, and among their children were Bennett's mother, Sarah Ann (1840–1914), and Frances Edna (died 1913), who married Ezra Bourne, a pottery manu-facturer. The Longson drapery shop was the model for the Baines shop in *The Old Wives' Tale,* and Frances Edna was the model for Auntie Hamps in the *Clay-hanger* trilogy. There were six surviving children in Bennett's immediate family. After Bennett himself came Frank (1868), Fanny Gertrude (1869), Emily Vernon (1871), Tertia (1872), and Septimus (1874).

Bennett wrote the following article for the *Daily Express,* where it appeared on 6 June 1928. It was one of a series by famous authors.

❧   ❧   ❧

It is said locally, with what truth I know not, that my family is descended on the paternal side from James Brindley, the eighteenth-century canal engineer – who used to be called "Schemer Brindley" in the Potteries, not because he intrigued but because he schemed schemes, chiefly for canals. The tale is that he made as many miles of canals as there are days in the year. He was apparently a genius; when he wanted to scheme he went to bed; he was illiterate, and had little use for such things as "working drawings" or written technical descriptions; he worked too hard and died too young. Doubt has been cast on his morals.

I can remember seeing my paternal grandfather once, when I was about three years of age. All that I know of him is that he was said to be the best "turner" in the pottery trade. This statement may have been true, or my grandfather may have been merely a fine "turner" upraised by family pride into the finest. He was a superior working-man, intensely respectable. He died young.

2

My paternal grandmother died before I first saw the smoke of the Potteries.

This grandfather had two sons and a daughter. The elder son was a pottery-painter. The Potteries being too small for him, he went to London, to a cottage in Lambeth. He exhibited a pottery-painting in his parlour window. Sir Henry Doulton, strolling that way, saw it, and engaged the artist for his Lambeth works.

Then, Doulton's being too small for him, my uncle migrated to America, where he succeeded and made money. Lambeth drew him back. He bought a row of cottages in Lambeth, which brought him in eighteen per cent on his capital. He lived in Lambeth in vigorous idleness for some years, and then returned to America, where he died.

He had a powerful, stimulating, and unconventional individuality. Full of more or less original ideas, he talked like an artist, and was one; but lack of education fatally vitiated his modes of thought, and his taste was, I fear, deplorable.

He and I often argued at length. We had trouble once when he insisted that Herkomer must be a great artist because he had uncompromisingly painted his father as an artisan. And once (1889) we quarrelled, when I told him straight that piano-lessons worth having could not be had at sixpence a time, the price he was paying. I apologised, but did not withdraw. He forgave.

His younger brother, my father, began, and failed, as a pottery manufacturer. Then he took to pawnbroking, and cared not for it. The pawnbroking establishment was transferred to his sister, my aunt, who conducted it for a long period. She was a tall, slim, auburn-haired, refined, and yet forceful woman, who had clear and personal ideas about books. She quarrelled with her fiancé, a plumber and an organist and a 'cellist, and, while living within a mile of him, never spoke to him for a dozen years or so. They then met again, married, and were perfectly happy ever after. They died within a couple of days of each other, at a great age, a year or two ago. Their sitting-room was behind the plumber's shop. The furniture of it was never altered.

My father was ambitious. At the age of nearly thirty, he did what to me has always seemed a marvellous thing – he decided to become a solicitor, and at the age of thirty-four he became one and set up in practice in the Potteries.

This was something of a feat for a man of his age, poor, and with a growing family. The three examinations must have put a terrible strain on him. He retired in 1900, when his health broke down, and died two years later. He admired the talents of his elder brother, and somewhat feared him, but condemned his unconventionalities. He was a strict teetotaler. He travelled twice, once to Paris and once to Scandinavia. Both these excursions were regarded as terrific, and so they were, for that time, and for a denizen of the Potteries.

Although he actually read little, beyond the usual Dickens and George Macdonald, he had a curious, detached interest in books, and his library was the largest in my youthful experience. I estimate it at a thousand volumes – mostly dull or worthless, but all dignified. He had a passion for filling his offspring with information, at small trouble to himself.

When any point of dispute arose he would say, "Look it up." We looked it up. He secretly thought that his children were the best behaved and the most gifted in the district, but to our faces he seldom praised us, and never without grave reserves. When I won twenty guineas for a short story in a weekly paper he said: "Well, it's better than a bat in the eye with a burnt stick." I took this for high laudation.

Often cheerful and vivacious, and much beloved, he was the complete autocrat at home. Napoleon at the Tuileries in 1806 was not more of an autocrat, nor better served. It was beneath his dignity to carry a latchkey. Arriving home, he would rap with his wedding-ring on the glass of the front door, and somebody scampered to open it, at no matter what hour.

I doubt whether his ambition survived intact his achievement of solicitorship. He had astonished the world, and was satisfied with that and with the reputation of being a sound lawyer. My chief recollection of him at home is an auburn-haired man lounging in an armchair in the dining-room, or sitting at the dining-room window. (He never used the drawing-room except to criticise his children's playing and singing.) In addition to being a disciplinarian, he loved to see others at work. Never would he allow his boys to go out and "play" in the evening like other boys. He relentlessly, ruthlessly, stimulated his children's ambitions, and his influence over us was immense, because he was keenly interested in us.

4

But the biggest individuality in my early experience was my maternal grandfather, tall, dark, moustacheless and bearded, who began life as a working weaver in Derbyshire. I remember him telling me that he would work at home twelve hours a day for five days, and on Saturday walk twelve miles with his week's weaving on his back to the town, sell the same, and walk home twelve miles with the money in his pocket. The seventh day was all chapel and Sunday school.

Later he set up as a draper in the Potteries, succeeded, and saved a lot more money, partly by unending small economies. His habits were austere and strict; but now and then he would go out to a public house and have a glass of beer on the quiet. He hated Gladstone, worshipped "Dizzy", read the *Standard*, looked on the *Daily Telegraph* as subversive, and confirmed me in Radicalism for life.

His wife, my grandmother, was an invalid, and suffered much with wondrous meekness and resignation. She died blind. He had two daughters and a son. The son was a faultless son. Of the daughters, the elder was my mother. The younger possessed one of the most powerful, attractive and formidable personalities I have ever encountered. She adored me, and burnt my first book in Wesleyan horror.

My mother during the lifetime of my father was my father's wife. But when he died we immediately discovered that she, too, had a most powerful individuality. She had also the great merit of being "interested in people". Her curiosity about them was inexhaustible, detached, and her judgment sound – if harsh. Nearly all her children were great humorists and teasers before the Lord, but she never in her life really saw a joke.

Often at family meals, when we were all adult and independent, I would commit some naughty witticism, and then, seeing her face, would walk round the table and kiss her. This reassured her. She read a lot, but only as most other people read, to pass the time. The mere mention of some of my books at table invariably caused her to play nervously with her bread.

I grew up in an atmosphere of sustained effort, of grim "sticking it", of silent endurance, of never being beaten by circumstances. I am now glad of it. But the atmosphere was also pietistic-religious, in a degree to me utterly exasperating. I spent large portions of time in being bored.

My compensations were, first, my father's ceaseless interest in my activities, and, second, the fact that in ceremonial religious matters my father did not practise what he preached.

When I was very young he gave up Sunday school entirely, and at no period did he attend chapel if he could decently help it. I objected to what I deemed his too stern treatment of us, but admired and was comforted by his aloof attitude towards dogmatic religion. Every mature person in my town-environment unendingly preached Christianity; but the number of those who regularly practised it in domestic life and in business could nearly be counted on the thumbs of two hands. At the age of forty or more I had to construct a religion of kindliness, forbearance, and the doctrines of the Mount for myself.

To conclude. Beyond doubt my father's influence was the main factor in making a home in which the "humanities" flourished more brightly than in any other home of my acquaintance. Entering the houses of his friends, wealthier or poorer, I always felt that I was going into something inferior, intellectually more confined and stuffy, places where the outlook was less wide and the dominant mentalities less vigorous, original, and free.

Earliest Dealings
with Literature

The following fragment from *The Truth About an Author* first appeared in the *Academy* on 3 May 1902. Bennett was by that time committed to a writing career. His chief income was as a reviewer and critic for the *Academy* and for *Hearth and Home*.

🐦 🐦 🐦

My dealings with literature go back, I suppose, some thirty and three years. We came together thus, literature and I. It was in a kitchen, at midday, and I was waiting for my dinner, hungry and clean, in a tartan frock with a pinafore over it. I had washed my own face, and dried it, and I remember that my eyes smarted with lingering soap, and my skin was drawn by the evaporation of moisture on a cold day. I held in my hand a single leaf which had escaped from a printed book. How it came into that chubby fist I cannot recall. The reminiscence begins with it already there. I gazed hard at the paper, and pretended with all my powers to be completely absorbed in its contents; I pretended to ignore some one who was rattling saucepans at the kitchen range. On my left a very long and mysterious passage led to a pawnshop all full of black bundles. I heard my brother crying at the other end of the passage, and his noisy naughtiness offended me. For myself, I felt excessively "good" with my paper; never since have I been so filled with the sense of perfect righteousness. Here was I, clean, quiet, sedate, studious; and there was my brother, the illiterate young Hooligan, disturbing the sacrosanct shop, and – what was worse – ignorant of his inferiority to me. Disgusted with him, I passed through the kitchen into another shop on the right, still conning the page with soapy, smarting eyes. At this point the light of memory is switched off. The printed matter, which sprang out of nothingness, vanishes back into the same.

I could not read, I could not distinguish one letter from another. I only knew that the signs and wonders constituted print, and I played at reading with intense earnestness. I actually felt learned, serious, wise, and competently superior, something like George Meredith's Dr Middleton. Would that I could identify this my very first literature! I review three or four hundred books annually now; out of crass, saccharine, sentimentality, I would give a year's harvest for the volume from which that leaf was torn, nay, for the leaf alone, as though it might be a Caxton. I remember that the paper was faintly bluish in tint, veined, and rather brittle. The book was probably printed in the eighteenth century. Perhaps it was Lavater's *Physiognomy* or Blair's *Sermons*, or Burnet's *Own Time*. One of these three, I fancy, it must surely have been.

After the miraculous appearance and disappearance of that torn leaf, I remember almost nothing of literature for several years. I was six or so when *The Ugly Duckling* aroused in me the melancholy of life, gave me to see the deep sadness which pervades all romance, beauty, and adventure. I laughed heartily at the old hen-bird's wise remark that the world extended past the next field and much further; I could perceive the humour of that. But when the ugly duckling at last flew away on his strong pinions, and when he met the swans and was accepted as an equal, then I felt sorrowful, agreeably sorrowful. It seemed to me that nothing could undo, atone for, the grief and humiliations of the false duckling's early youth. I brooded over the injustice of his misfortunes for days, and the swans who welcomed him struck me as proud, cold, and supercilious in their politeness. I have never read *The Ugly Duckling* since those days. It survives in my memory as a long and complex narrative, crowded with vague and mysterious allusions, and wet with the tears of things. No novel – it was a prodigious novel for me – has more deliciously disturbed me, not even *On the Eve* or *Lost Illusions*. Two years later I read *Hiawatha*. The picture which I formed of Minnehaha remains vividly and crudely with me; it resembles a simpering waxen doll of austere habit. Nothing else can I recall of *Hiawatha*, save odd lines, and a few names such as Gitchee-Gumee. I did not much care for the tale. Soon after I read it, I see a vision of a jolly-faced house-painter graining a door. "What do you call that?" I asked him, pointing to some very peculiar piece of graining, and he replied, gravely: "That, young sir, is a wigwam to wind the moon up with." I privately decided that he must have read, not *Hiawatha*, but something similar and stranger, something even more wig-wammy. I dared not question him further, because he was so witty . . .

How I Was Educated

Bennett attended the Burslem Wesleyan Day School probably during 1875 and 1876, the Burslem Endowed School from 1877 to April 1882, and the Newcastle Middle School from May 1882 to the end of 1883. He was top of Forms V and VI at the Burslem Endowed School, and became head boy at the New-castle Middle School. He left the Middle School to enter his father's law office. He failed his legal examinations in 1887 and again in 1888. In March 1889 he came to London to be a shorthand clerk in the law offices of Le Brasseur & Oakley, where he remained until the end of 1893.

The following article appeared in *John O'London's Weekly* on 28 June 1930. A few sentences have been omitted that repeat comments in "The Making of Me".

༄ༀ   ༄ༀ   ༄ༀ

At school I was chiefly bored. I went to three schools. The first is not worth mentioning. The second is hardly worth mentioning. The headmaster introduced the horizontal bar, singlestick, bronze medals (I lost mine – for arithmetic), and marching into school and out of school to a tune of his own playing on a harmonium. The third was better: a fair average "middle" school (endowed).

English grammar was well taught at this school. So were

French grammar and very elementary Latin grammar. Geography was well taught, though on old-fashioned lines. I have remembered the grammars and the geography, and they have always been very useful to me. The teaching of English history was preposterous: a silly system and tedious textbooks, resulting in knowledge both misleading and comically partial. No foreign history whatever was taught. Chemistry and all physics were very badly taught.

In the department of literature, no attempt was apparent to make literature interesting, or even to explain its aim, its beauty, and its relation to life. Shakespeare was cut up alive into specimens of sixteenth century locutions. And why a cardinal and delicate poet like Virgil, or any poet, should have been chosen to illustrate the peculiarities of a dead language I cannot conceive. Julius Caesar alone coherently survived the processes to which he was subjected. But then no pedagogy could kill the sturdy prose of Caesar. French was taught as a dead language, with the aid of the most fatuous sentimental fiction and dull biographies of military heroes.

I had supplementary lessons in "art", being taught to "draw" by the copying of elaborate Renaissance designs in pencil! There was absolutely nothing in the curriculum to stimulate the imagination or the faculty of observation. Games were the usual games; and I played them but was inimical to them. The school had a good reputation, doubtless deserved, according to contemporary standards. I despised it for a strange reason – namely, because, well aware that I knew nothing, I nevertheless rose with extraordinary rapidity to the top of the school. I thought: "If I am captain of this school, what a rotten school it must be, and what rotters must be the other boys!"

I left school at sixteen (1883). I at once sat for the London Matric., and passed. Perhaps the stupidity of the Matric. examination-papers explained the stupidities of the educational system partly designed to lead up to them. The French paper in particular was a marvel of ineptitude. Two or three years later I sat for the London LL.B. Intermediate. Three subjects, and you had to pass in all of them. I failed in all of them. I sat again, and failed in one of them. This comi-tragedy finished my "education", which had included not a single lesson on, or even reference to, the master-theory of evolution; neither any guidance to the philosophy of conduct.

Withal, I did learn valuable matters in my studies for the LL.B. Intermediate. Maine's *Ancient Law* was among the books "set". It awoke my imagination, showed a little how to think from cause to effect, and rendered certain aspects of antique life more real to me than the Battle of Hastings or Magna Carta. And school, I admit, had taught me something more valuable than grammar and geography. It had taught me how to keep to a time-table, to be in a certain place at a certain hour, and to complete (more or less) a certain task by a certain hour – and no nonsense permitted! . . .

The seed of the lesson did not fall on stony ground. I grew more and more addicted to the organization of my time. The consequence was that I have acquired an unmerited reputation for being a hard worker. I am not a hard worker; I am merely an organized worker. I have not worked in the evening more than a couple of times in twenty years, and I have regularly slept after lunch for a quarter of a century. And I am seldom or never in a hurry. I say to people: "I must go now." They say: "You are always in a hurry." It is untrue. I am only maintaining my schedule. And yet I was over fifty before I discovered that an odd half-hour, unexpectedly intervening between two tasks, need not be cast away profitless into the abyss of eternity! Since then, in odd half-hours suddenly thrown to me by the vagaries of men and circumstance, I have considerably advanced even long books, which many authors will not touch unless they feel sure of at least three uninterrupted hours. I wish that I had made this wonderful discovery much earlier in life.

As regards my self-education, as distinguished from the education imposed on me, it began, feebly, at the age of twenty-one, when I quitted the romance of the Potteries for the prose of London. I learnt to speak German – and in course of time entirely lost this pleasing faculty, through disuse of it. And I learnt to read Italian – and lost this faculty too. French I acquired permanently. Four or five years in the office of London lawyers enabled me to learn a bit about human nature. And four or five years in weekly journalism forced me to learn how to capture by words the attention of the average man – a personage, let me say, whom I deeply respect.

But what more than anything else helped me to help myself in education was the frequenting of artists in other arts: painters, designers, sculptors, musicians. These friends and acquaintances unconsciously indicated to me other ways of seeing and feeling than the ways employed in literature. They enlarged the boundaries of my vision, my emotions, and my curiosity. I have learnt little from the companionship of authors. Indeed, up to the age of forty I knew very few authors and few journalists.

How did I learn to write? I didn't. I am still learning to write, and by the only method. You learn to write by writing and writing and writing; but you must take each word by itself, examining it as you would examine a criminal, and by avoiding ready-made phrases. There is no harder work than learning to write. It is so hard that it prevents general "education" in the customary sense of the term. But the novelist, who has to deal with everything in life, has a great privilege. He is permitted to have no exact knowledge of anything in life – except his craft, and not always that.

School-Days in the Five Towns

The following essay was published in *Youth's Companion* in America in September 1915 and in the *Windsor Magazine* in December 1916. Several sentences have been omitted from the opening that repeat comments in "The Making of Me" and "How I Was Educated". The song from *Milestones* that Bennett alludes to is "Juanita".

౿ఇ   ౿ఇ   ౿ఇ

I cannot remember ever getting any pleasure out of the great official enterprise of learning. I never enjoyed school, and I assuredly never enjoyed home-lessons. Not until I was nearly forty did it suddenly occur to me that getting knowledge was in itself rather fun, and not a tedious means to a desirable end. Nor had I, I believe, even any genuine pride in the mediocre achievements of my school career. I scorned them. My brother also scorned them. One exception is to be made to this generalisation. When we were exceedingly young – for schoolboys – my father used to hold a sort of competition, tournament, or joust of knowledge in the dining-room after high tea on Saturday afternoons. We looked forward to this solemnity as eagerly as two terriers to a ratting. Our nostrils twitched for it. The competition included the whole field of knowledge. My father would pose a question, and the child who first answered it received one mark. In practice the answer had to be instantaneous in order to stand a chance of winning

14

a mark. And, to be fair, my father ought to have had a stop-watch showing fifths of a second. But instead of a stop-watch he relied on his ear and on his autocratic authority. The questions were simple. And yet a certain amount of nerve and presence of mind must have been needed to decide instantly, for example, whether the cube of 4 is greater or less than the square of 8, or whether the Battle of Bannockburn occurred in 1314 or 1413. At the close of the joust the marks were added up, and the victor received the sum of one penny – to do what he liked with, except buy sweets. In time, of course, we outgrew my father's capacity to preside with *éclat* at these tournaments, and they ceased. And then ceased my sole delight in erudition.

As regards my own private enterprises in boyhood, they were not greatly concerned with games. I played almost no football until after I had left school. There were no facilities whatever in our district for aquatic sports, save swimming; and I became very fond of swimming, but I had left school before I could swim a stroke. I had no interest in cricket until I was turned thirty, and none after I was thirty-five. The games which could interest me even faintly were the simple and truly ancient games needing little apparatus, or none at all, such as tick, tip-cat, prison-bars, leap-frog, and rounders. I believe that some of these games are now extinct. Tip-cat was a very favourite game, and, I still think, a good one. The entire apparatus for it would cost far less than a single golf ball. I also had a considerable passion for kites, probably because we had to make our own kites or do without kites. I remember that at one period croquet held us like a religion. Some big and magnificent boys and girls next door played croquet with genuine croquet mallets and croquet balls on a genuine lawn. Myself and my tribe manufactured croquet balls out of pebbles and rags, and mallets out of I forget what, and hoops out of twigs, and thus played our own passionate croquet.

When I was young I had no consciousness of being interested in the arts, yet I was. Before I went to school I was a feverish water-colourist. I painted lovely moss roses on glossy white cards, and then, discovering that moss roses and white cards were commonplace, I went into sepia and landscapes and drawing-blocks. There was then something peculiarly distinguished about sepia . . . I had an aunt who generously patronised the artist in me.

This aunt was affianced to a young widower, who, in the intervals of manufacturing pottery, also painted landscapes in sepia. Indeed, I expect that it was he who first infected me with the sepia virus. He was, I opined, a miraculous artist, and he would lend me his visions to copy. I copied them with a singular correctness of draughtsmanship, if not of tint. He was a suspicious and an observant man, and about to become my uncle. He held up one of his own drawings to the light, and noticed that at every important point of the design there was a pin-prick. The truth was that I had laid his drawings, sacred to my aunt, flat on my blank drawing-paper, and pricked off the principal features as a guide to my pencil. Some slight unpleasantness followed the exposure, and my recollection is that sepia languished.

We passed to music – my brother, two sisters, and myself. Some relative taught us our notes, and no more, and we were left free with a piano and a popular book of instruction written by a person named Hemy. We soon grew sick of Hemy. And our passion for hymn tunes did not endure. There remained a miscellaneous pile of songs and "pieces", mostly either dull or unplay-able. Apart from anything inside the covers of Hemy, the two masterpieces of musical composition were "The Carnival of Venice" – with variations – and "Silvery Waves". We ultimately grew sick of these two. Then came the great vital episode of the loan by the aforesaid aunt of a bound volume of unknown and undreamt-of songs and "pieces". Among the songs was the pathetic ballad which I remembered nearly forty years later and suggested to my collaborator, Edward Knobloch, for the first and third acts of *Milestones*. He jumped at it. All Victoria's reign is in the air of that ballad.

Among the "pieces" was "The Osborne Quadrilles", for pianoforte duet. Now, we knew not that we could play pianoforte duets. We sat down to try, and we found that we could. An epoch was marked. Within the day we could rattle off those quadrilles with the assurance of a modern pianola. We were exquisitely staggered by our own gifts, our parents rather more so, and even our parents' friends not less so. For remember, "The Osborne Quadrilles" were not Hemy, neither were they hymn tunes, nor "The Carnival of Venice", nor "Silvery Waves". They were music – unfamiliar, adult, splendid.

We subscribed to a penny musical weekly – or perhaps it was a twopenny – which consisted of simplified extracts from the music of all times and climes. We were taken – occasionally – to grand concerts given by travelling troupes. My sisters sang. I believe I sang myself. My younger brother, having shown what were believed to be unusual gifts, "had lessons" on the pianoforte, and passed upwards out of our sight into the empyrean. I then took up the fiddle. But the tragedy was cut short by a doctor, who in lancing the forefinger of my left hand, lanced part of the machinery of the finger, which has never been able to bend itself since. I relinquished the fiddle, and have thenceforward consistently posed as a genius victimised by evil chance. But the doctor, having once heard me play the fiddle, may have done what he did on purpose! I returned to pianoforte duets, which to this day remain for me the most sporting form of sport.

I had no traffic with other arts. I did keep a diary for three days when I was about seven years of age, and I did write a story in my early school-days, but I assuredly displayed no reasonable interest in literature until after I had left school.

As a boy my traffic with the arts was adventurous, and was so regarded by me; but of adventure, or even longing for adventure, in the usual sense of the term, I had little or none. In particular, I had no desire to go to sea or to the pathless forest. And Five Towns boys were not allowed much travelling then. When an infant I had the enormous luck to go several times alone with my grandmother to Buxton. She was losing, and had nearly lost, her eyesight. I was her guide. Once, in passing a post-office, she exclaimed excitedly: "I can read the words 'Post Office'!" These were, perhaps, the last words she ever did read. The extreme pathos of this did not strike me. But the immense romance of going to Buxton struck me. Buxton was twenty-five miles off, and you had to "change". I vividly recall the seductive smell of cookery coming up from the basement kitchens of Buxton boarding-houses. And Buxton is still a most romantic spot for me.

After Buxton I had no travel for a long time, except the annual family excursions to the seaside, which, though attractive and not to be despised, were conventional affairs marred by discipline. When I was promoted from the purely local school to a historic establishment in the educational town of Newcastle, the walk morning and evening between Burslem and Newcastle, across a marsh and past coalpits and ponds, and over a canal and a railway or so, had in a high degree the quality of adventure. It was three miles in length, and had the interminableness of thirty. Further, the school "tuck shop" was kept by a Frenchwoman, slatternly and talkative and a good pastry-maker. She, too, was romantic for me. The misguided lady once told me that the word *insulte* was masculine. I accepted her authority, and made the word *insulte* masculine for thirty years, and when at last I was corrected by another Frenchwoman, it needed the dictionary to convince me, and I could hardly believe the dictionary! Such is the force of dogma implanted in infancy!

The capital adventure of my later school-days was the annual Easter walk on Easter Monday. It was generally to Buxton, because Buxton conserved its romance. We went off in a band, girls and boys, and, taking train at intervals, would do about twenty-five miles walking in the day. The crown of the terrific day was a supper of celestial ham and eggs at home at the close of it. One year the walk was postponed to Whitsuntide. We were very lively, and had energy enough to do some swimming at Buxton. When we left Buxton, we had exactly three hours to cover the thirteen miles from Buxton to Leek Station – and a hilly road. We did it, girls as well as boys – and the last five miles in an hour! Then we had ten miles of train, and finally two miles more to walk. It was the last two miles, in the dark, that killed us. The repose in the train stiffened our joints so that we could hardly get out of the train. The two miles, over a hill, were appalling. Still, the heavenly thought of ham and eggs cheered us. We reached home. We bathed. We smelt the smell of the traditional ham and eggs. We tried to think "How lovely!" We sat down to table. We tried nobly to eat . . . We could not! We were too tired to swallow! We went to bed of our own accord. This was a tragedy, and a true tragedy. I shall never forget it. We had no more grand ceremonial walks. Moreover, my school-days were finished.

A Visit from Mr Hurley

D. B. Hurley (1844–1919) was headmaster of the
Newcastle Middle School from 1879 to 1906. He
visited Bennett in 1908 at Bennett's new home near
Fontainebleau. Bennett was recently married to a
Frenchwoman, Marguerite Soulié, and was probably
just finished with the writing of *The Old Wives' Tale*.
M. D. Calvocoressi (1877–1944) was a close friend
of Bennett's, and had introduced him to Marguerite.

Bennett wrote the following sketch in December
1909 for publication in the *Median*, the magazine of the
Middle School.

꒰ꕤ꒱   ꒰ꕤ꒱   ꒰ꕤ꒱

I was consuming tea with my wife and some friends, in the
drawing-room of my house at Fontainebleau, when the fore-part
of a bicycle and the fore-part of a man came peeping round the
angle of the house in at the open French window. The bicycle, so
far as I know, had no thrilling interest, but the man was Mr
D. B. Hurley, headmaster of our school during a whole generation.
It must be quite a quarter of a century since I left the school,
and in the long interval I had not seen very much of Mr Hurley.
This arrival, that afternoon at Fontainebleau, was an exciting
surprise, though I knew him to be wheeling about somewhere
in France, and had received a letter from him.

The sight of him "gave me to think". I naturally thought of his cane, which more than once in its breezy style had chanced to collide somewhat brusquely with the palm of my hand, and I thought of sundry human beings who had faded, or were fading, from my memory. Leek, for instance. Leek was head boy when I fluttered tremblingly into the Lower Sixth. He had a prodigious reputation as a classical scholar and I shall always think of him, with his fair hair and taciturn manner, as the greatest classical scholar that ever crossed the Ironmarket. Then there was Mellard. Mellard was like the cane, breezy, and an outdoor youth. He went forth to be either a pirate or a pilot on the Hoogli (excuse me if I have failed in the spelling of this tortuous river: I never could spell it), and there was Jack Booth, a fine cricketer (though not equal to his lesser brother George), and always very "decent" with small boys, whom he could easily have flung over a hedge, and the gigantic Ernest Walker, of whom it was said in awe that he could hit half-a-crown with a catapult at twenty yards (not that I ever saw him do it), and Marshall, a highly agreeable crony, who for some deep reason (never explained) was called "the Sunday" by his intimates; and Hughes, and Tommy Warrington, a terrific worker. I thought of these and lots more, and I reflected that some of them might be dead, and some might be grandfathers, and that certainly not one of them could be less than forty.

Here was the man who had been headmaster before even the eldest of them had reached the sixth, skimming airily up my garden on a bicycle! In the early eighties I used to regard Mr Hurley as an old man, with one foot in the grave (and the other twisted round his famous stool). I can perceive what a ghastly mistake I had then made; for the truth is that he was much younger than I was myself. His hair, no doubt, was grizzled, but his gestures, his vivacity, and his intense interest in everything belied his hair; and I don't know how many kilometres he had pedalled that day! He called me "boy" in exactly the tone of a quarter of a century earlier, but by the side of his magnificent energy I felt doddering, and I can assure you privately that I shall never see forty-two again.

Everybody who knows Mr Hurley knows that the chief hobby of his life has been, and is, foreign languages. Now it occurred that in my house this hobby had full scope for a gallop – a fair field and no favours. My wife is a Southern Frenchwoman of the purest extraction. Also there was present a young lady who had so far been educated in Germany that she would dream in German, and further, there was my friend M. D. Calvocoressi, the well-known Parisian musical critic on the staff of *Gil Blas*, who is one of the three greatest linguists I have ever met. You may see on the title pages of Russian songs, published in Paris, London and Leipzig, these words: "Translated into English verse by M. D. Calvocoressi." "Translated into French verse by M. D. Calvocoressi." "Translated into German verse by M. D. Calvocoressi." A man who can translate Russian into the verse of three different foreign languages may indeed call himself a linguist. Madame Calvocoressi, his mother, was also present. When my friend and his mother talk between themselves they use Greek, for they are both Greek. Into such an assembly came the linguist from North Staffordshire. I said to myself: "we shall now see whether Mr Hurley is really equal to his immense local reputation."

He was.

He was far more than equal to it. He shone, and I was extremely proud of him. The conversation naturally became linguistic, and Mr Hurley was ready to chat with anybody, about anything, in any language. Like him, Mr Calvocoressi is passionately interested in idioms, argot, and peculiar constructions and laws of phrase. They talked, these two! They came to grips. If it was not a case of Greek meeting Greek, it was a case of Greek meeting Irishman! (Mr Hurley "had" them all there, by the way; he could use a tongue which none of them understood – ancient Irish!) When each of us had to cite examples of French sentences which are difficult to enunciate rapidly, it was Mr Hurley who spreadeagled the field. I may as well give you his champion sentence. SI CES SIX CENT SIX SANGSUES SONT SUR SON SEIN SANS SUCER SON SANG, CES SIX CENT SIX SANGSUES SONT SANS SUCCÈS. Try it. It is unrivalled for dyspepsia, neuralgia and appendicitis. Later, Mr Hurley and Mr Calvocoressi began discussing Greek roots. They went out for a walk together, still discussing Greek roots. I went upstairs to my couch to seek a few moments mental repose.

Mr Hurley spent the night with us. He invigorated the whole house by his youthfulness. The next morning I heard him playing the piano long before I was in a position to descend; and when I did come down he unrolled before me an even vaster panorama of his multifarious interests in life, and in the lives of other people. It seemed to me that he could recall the names and histories of about ten million different boys. Incidentally, he was good enough to present me with a copy of a learned edition of a German classic which he had edited. Unfortunately I was unable to keep him more than twenty-four hours. He was inevitably bound for Paris.

I never found enough courage to confide to him that for over a quarter of a century I had borne one single solitary grudge against him. It arose from a difficulty that I had with the Reverend Ambrose Pope, who, I am glad to see from the last number of the *Median*, has taken that exceedingly difficult and rare degree, "D.Lit.Lond." Twenty-six years ago or thereabouts, Mr Pope was the youngest master. I was head boy. There cannot have been more than a few years between our ages. Mr Pope told me to do something. I considered that in giving an order to a head-boy Mr Pope was going rather far. I considered that a request would have been more discreet than an order; and I defied Mr Pope. I was of course completely in the wrong. I hadn't a leg to stand on. The drama had a rather painful last act in Mr Hurley's dreaded private room, into which Mr Pope and I penetrated together. "Will you take a seat, Mr Pope?" said Mr Hurley. He didn't ask *me* to sit down, and it was not quite nice of him, seeing that I hadn't a leg to stand on.

Alone in London

In *The Truth About an Author* Bennett says, "I came to London at the age of twenty-one, with no definite ambition, and no immediate object save to escape from an intellectual and artistic environment which had long been excessively irksome to me." He wrote the following two articles some fourteen years later, and he had long since taken the advice that the articles recommended to others. The first of the articles is negligible except for the sense it gives of Bennett the ordinary man who neither in 1903 nor at any later time felt that the ordinary thoughts and desires of other men were beneath his interest and concern. He himself found a circle of convivial friends fairly soon upon his arrival in London. They included Joseph Hill, founder and director of the Blackheath School of Art, Herbert Sharpe, professor at the Royal Academy of Music, and Frederick Marriott, art master at Goldsmiths' College. At the offices of Le Brasseur & Oakley he found another friend, John Eland, who was a collector of books, and Eland and Bennett spent many hours together in the search for books that the second article describes. One consequence of their search along the Farringdon Road and elsewhere was that in 1891 and again in 1892 Bennett issued catalogues of rare and unusual books for sale. A later consequence was that when he wrote *Riceyman Steps* in 1922–3 he chose Clerkenwell district for the home of his bookseller-hero.

The two articles were part of a series of seven articles of advice to the young man alone in London, and they elicited many letters from readers. The others concerned such matters as clothing and lodging. All of them were part of a longer series of "Savoir-Faire Papers", by "The Man Who Does". The series ran in *T.P.'s Weekly* from 14 November 1902 to 6 November 1903.

ᴜ🐦   ᴜ🐦   ᴜ🐦

Alone in London - I

The young man alone in London soon makes the surprising discovery that he is lonely. At first, and for some weeks or months after his arrival, he keeps the hope that things are going to alter, and that in due course he will find himself in a social circle of congenial brilliance. He does not see clearly how this desired result is to be brought about, but, on the other hand, he cannot contemplate a future in which it has not been brought about. The idea that he will always remain thus solitary is monstrous and unthinkable to him, and he continues to nurse his hope. Meanwhile, the months slip by and the years slip by; and he falls into the habits of solitude. He may have become familiar with a man at the office who is tolerable, and the man at the office may have a sister who would be tolerable if— But, on the whole, he lives in crowded London like a hermit. He makes little excursions by himself on Saturdays and Sundays; he kills his evenings in study or in "messing about"; he unconsciously gesticulates and talks as he passes along the street. And when at length he has discovered and admitted that things will always be like this, he persuades himself that it is better so, and that he is by nature of a solitary disposition; he even tries to persuade himself that he prefers the hermit's career. But occasionally, in the long evenings, he gets sentimental, and feels sorry for his sensitive soul, and constructs a philosophy which is half cynicism and half Clifton Bingham or F. E. Weatherly.

But what did this young man expect? Did he expect to find London a delightful maze of intersecting brilliant social circles?

Did he really expect that London is fundamentally different from Basingstoke or Blackburn? And did he really and truly expect that congenial friends would by some miracle present themselves at the door of his bed-sitting-room while he waited supinely for their magic arrival? Friendships are not achieved that way. Any fool can earn a living without perspiring too much; but to make friends that are worth making means hard work; it is a manufacturing operation not to be performed by strolling up and down the Embankment on a moonlight night, musing upon the stony indifference of a great city.

The young man's preconceived notions are all wrong, and his plan of action, or, rather, his plan of inactivity, is all wrong. The young man of ideas comes to London and vaguely expects to find it pretty full of interesting, outstanding individualities. But the percentage of interesting individualities in average London is probably less than in any decent provincial town. Interesting individualities come to London; and a few – a very few – are born there. But many of them leave it as soon as they have fully flowered, and most of the rest congregate together as soon as they have fully flowered, and keep themselves to themselves. The raw provincial has no chance of seeing them. Consequently, although special parts of London, special circles in London, coruscate with attractive cleverness, the vast generality of London is commonplace, dull, and lacking in any salience, to a perfectly extraordinary degree. Nevertheless, friends can be made there.

But not by solitary "mooning". The mistakes the lonely young man makes are two. He doesn't put himself to any real trouble in the quest of friends, and he is infinitely too particular in his choice at the beginning. He might as well expect to walk down the Strand and pick up a sovereign opposite Short's as expect to find an entirely suitable friend at the first essay. The colleague in the office doesn't care for literature, or takes the wrong side in politics, or in neckties, or speaks with a bad accent, or has a bad temper, and so my lonely young man lifts his nose and snorts at the colleague in the office. Which is very foolish of my lonely young man. And it is foolish because of the great truth, especially great in this business of friend-finding, that "one thing leads to another".

All that the lonely desirer of friends should need is a "jumping-off point". And the colleague at the office will answer this purpose almost as well as a more congenial individual. Do not, young man, ignore the colleague at the office because you are not wildly pleased with him. If he is the only person you happen to know, cultivate him. Among the people he knows may be an individuality which interests you. And if not, you have but to continue the progression. Among the people known by the people that he knows there may be an individuality which is interesting to you; or among the people known by the people known by the people that he knows! Once started, once determined, the desirer of friends has, in the ultimate result, the whole of London for his hunting ground. He may not enjoy the immediate acquaintance of the Right Honourable Joseph Chamberlain M.P., or the Disappearing Lady Doctor; but he doubtless knows someone who knows someone who knows someone – (continue sufficiently) – who knows these exalted and piquant personages.

And there are other "jumping-off points" besides the colleague at the office – jumping-off points connected with lawn tennis clubs, churches, polytechnic institutes, political and ethical societies, philharmonic societies, Mr Stead's meetings, and what not. I need scarcely describe them; their characteristics and possibilities are sufficiently well known. What is desiderated is, not opportunities, but the enterprise to use them, and to use them at once with persistency and with discretion. I would submit the following three maxims or wise saws, specially invented for this occasion, to the consideration of the lonely young man who has discovered that congenial friends do not precisely besiege his door:

1. Avoid fastidiousness; it is almost always necessary to submit to boredom in order to arrive at the state of not being bored.

2. Persevere; you may have to undergo fifty banal introductions before finding one single friend.

3. It is kinder, both to him and to you, to drop instantly an acquaintance who has proved useless. Men rise on stepping-stones of their dropped acquaintances to more congenial things.

A man (unless he is very abnormally afflicted by shyness) gets the friends he deserves. And if after years of expectancy he finds himself practically solus in a place like London, he may with perfect confidence call himself either a ninny, a coward, or a boor.

Some men, by natural gifts of charm or insight into character, make friends with less preliminary trouble than others. But all men can make friends if they will persevere and refrain from being too severely eclectic in the way of small things.

I must touch on a final point; namely, that in London the two sexes do not sufficiently mix. Many young men have a fairly wide circle of friends, but it is an exclusively masculine circle. Many young women have a fairly wide circle of friends, but it is an exclusively feminine circle. Such a state of affairs is bad in every way. It is not the fault of the women, but of the men. There is an idea rooted in the heart of the young man that the young woman over the garden wall or in the next row at the polytechnic is well satisfied with the society of her own sex; that she would be rather stand-offish if he approached her; and that she does not, in fact, as he does, yearn for the mild romance of "mixed" companionship. Never was a rooted idea more preposterous. Excellent young man, she is just like you, only more so. The chances are ten thousand to one that she longs to improve the acquaintance much more than you do. You see, she has fewer distractions.

Alone in London - II

The individual alone in London has a special need for books. It is only the solitary man who really appreciates the full significance of that extraordinary word *book*. Books he must have, books he must understand, and books he must love – or it will be better for him that he had never been born, or at least that he had stayed in Little Pedlington and married the draper's pale daughter. In this periodical there is no need for me to offer any apology for attaching a particular importance to books, but I cannot forbear to draw the attention of those who do not traffic regularly with books to the magnificent eulogy, apology, and defence of books and their authors, in the tenth chapter of Mr H. G. Wells's new work, *Mankind in the Making*. It is the most passionate thing in that line that I remember to have seen, and deserves to be read solemnly aloud in places (whether bed-sitting-rooms or spacious homes) where the purchase of books is not a usual weekly business. Of course Mr Wells is slightly "above himself" in advocating that we should devote so monstrous a sum as a million a year to the national endowment of authors (seeing that we are spending a mere ninety millions a year on our army), but what writer will not get above himself in the heat and splendour of a fine moment? The mention of ninety millions reminds me that in my last paper I suggested that the average young man alone in London should spend on literature annually the sum of four pounds (out of a total of a hundred and twenty). He may enquire, "What can be done with £4?" A great deal, if you go the right way about it.

In the first place, it is necessary to enlarge one's notions of the book market. The average man's notion of the book market is a beautiful shop-window, with rows of beautiful new books in speckless and variegated cloth bindings, and complete sets of established authors in morocco, calf, and russia, and large illustrated volumes opened temptingly at a picture, and editions de luxe dotted about, and vistas of the Temple Classics in leather just to give a contrast to the portliness of the rest. And inside the shop, which is as religiously dim as a church, are all the latest things, and polished assistants incessantly engaged in taking twenty-five per cent off six shillings. Mr Morley's *Life of Gladstone* is there, three volumes, price two guineas net, and Blowitz's *My Memoirs*, price fifteen shillings net; and Mr Kipling's *The Five Nations*, price six shillings; and the *Correspondence of William I and Bismarck,* two volumes, price one pound net; and *Barlasch of the Guard,* by Mr Henry Seton Merriman, price six shillings, all books which it is imperative to have read . . . and lo! the four pounds is more than gone! . . . Well, that is certainly part of the book market, and those books (some of them) are certainly a part of literature, but just such part as the book-buyer of limited means, and the book-lover who has a broad view of literature, should leave alone. My young man must not enter a new book-shop to spend more than half-a-crown on a book, and not often to spend more than a shilling. He must also get firmly fixed into his head the indubitable truth that it is advantageous to keep oneself quite a year behind contemporary literature; this rearwardness saves both time and money. And, further, he must continually dwell on the relative unimportance of contemporary literature compared to the whole of literature: it is only contemporary literature that is dear.

As a violent contrast to the richness of the new-book emporium in the Strand or Cheapside, and by way of initiating him into the methods of the cheapest book-buying, I will conduct my young man eastwards. Let him visit Farringdon Road, Aldgate, and Shoreditch, and gaze upon the thousands of books there displayed on barrows in the street. (There are other book-barrow streets in London, but these three are the best.) He will find that the prices of books commence here at a halfpenny apiece and go up to a shilling apiece; a shilling is princely. Now about ninety-nine per cent of these books will be useless to the man of literary taste, but the remaining one per cent will not be useless. I should estimate that there are always at least five thousand books displayed for sale in Farringdon Road alone, which means, according to my theory, that there are always fifty books worth buying there – provided one wants them. Of course these books need to be carefully searched for; and of course the man who knows most about literature is the most likely not to overlook them. English and foreign classics are always to be got there. Let it be also remembered that some books are worth buying merely as furniture, for their bindings. I have acquired some pretty bindings in the East End, and some useful works of reference, and not a few of the rarer English classics. I well remember the first "bargain" I got in Farringdon Road. It was *The Golden Remains of the Ever-memorable John Hale,* one shilling. I sold it for five shillings to an eminent Q.C., M.P., because he wanted it more than I did. My advice to the incipient book-buyer is to spend a trial Saturday afternoon in the districts I have mentioned, and see how he likes it. He may fail, but, on the other hand, he may return with two or three useful, rare, or handsome volumes (a shilling the lot), and be strongly encouraged to go again.

I should point out that the man who seriously takes to book-buying, even inexpensive book-buying, is seldom content to remain a purchaser of books for the purpose of reading. He develops into a purchaser of books as curiosities, and his library grows into a museum, as well as a storehouse of ideas. In other words, he becomes a book-*collector*. This branch of book-buying is as complex and difficult as it is interesting. The tyro should obtain Mr J. H. Slater's *Books and Book-collecting*, which will serve to put him on the right path.

Another resort of the book-buyer of limited means is Charing Cross Road (which has taken the place of the demolished Book-sellers' Row). The books displayed on the external shelves here are not as cheap as the contents of the street barrows; but, to compensate, the proportion of books worth buying is much larger. There are few days on which a shilling cannot be very profitably spent in Charing Cross Road. Second-hand French novels usually abound. The last book I bought there was Loti's *Pêcheur d'Islande*: it was clean, and cost me one shilling instead of three. A good rule, by the way, is to resist all temptation to purchase any book that is not both clean and "perfect". If it is dirty, if it lacks a page – leave it, no matter what air it has of being a bargain.

To return to contemporary literature The man who has "no use for" old books, rare books, books with beautiful exteriors, but who wants books nevertheless, should get the "remainder" catalogues of Mr Glashier (Holborn). Here he will find many recent and quite new books (some of them most excellent and desirable) which are marked at low prices because the publishers have failed to get rid of their stocks. He may also demand the second-hand catalogues of Messrs Mudie and Messrs Smith and Son, from whom he can buy, six months or so after publication, almost any new novel, say, at about a third of the original price. Such copies are, of course, not "new"; they have been through the mill of the circulating library. Messrs Smith's copies are superior to those of Messrs Mudie, because the latter paste their label on the outside of the book, whereas the former secrete the horrid thing on the inside front-cover. Lastly, I shall allow my book-buyer to enter the gorgeous new-book-shop occasionally, and buy some tasteful, well-edited, inexpensive edition of an immortal work, or some new work that he feels he can't do without, straight from the polished assistant. Asked how many books he should be able to acquire annually with his four pounds, I answer: Fifty at least; perhaps seventy-five; it depends on his luck and his skill.

Editing a Woman's Paper

Bennett became assistant editor of *Woman* in January 1894, at a starting salary of £150 a year. In the three preceding years he published occasional miscellaneous items in the London press, beginning with a prize story in *Tit-Bits* in December 1891 and including brief articles on legal matters. With a single exception, none of this writing was of any distinction, and Bennett estimated later than he earned threepence an hour in producing it. The exception was the story "A Letter Home", which he wrote in 1893 with a high artistic aim in mind and which the high-class *Yellow Book* published in 1895. His pseudonyms on *Woman* included Barbara, Sarah Volatile, Jim's Wife, and Cecile. He also wrote as Sarah Volatile in *Hearth and Home*, and in 1898 he gave favourable notice to his first novel, *A Man from the North*, under the name of Sarah Volatile in the latter paper, and brother Frank reviewed it favourably under the name Frances in *Woman*.

The following article was published in *Harper's Bazaar* in August 1927. The ellipses indicate omission of miscellaneous general comments on women in the 1890s.

Woman was a penny illustrated weekly paper for women, and I became the editor of it in November 1896, at the tender age of twenty-nine. Although then, as now, I kept a Journal, it was chiefly impressionistic, and not a diary of facts, and I can find only one entry in it which bears on the sublime fact of my ascent to the throne. The entry runs:

> Today a business crisis which has been active for a fortnight ended with a definite arrangement that I should accept the editorship. A fortnight of secret conclaves suddenly hushed at the sound of a door opening, of poring over figures and lists of names and correspondence; of devising schemes, each one superseded by a better, a more perfect one; of planning and counter-planning; of saying the same thing over and over again to a colleague, merely because it was impossible to leave the subject and impossible to say anything fresh; of publicly expressed hopes and private pessimisms; of forced jocularities; of feverish incessant *thinking* by day and by night, awake and asleep, walking or sitting, silent or speaking. Almost my first real taste of a strictly business personal anxiety! A few years of such anxiety (the lot of many men), even a year of it, even a month, would drive me, I fancy to clerkhood again.

(No, it wouldn't.)

I was young, but I had not the slightest idea that I was young. I thought I was quite old. . . . I ought to mention I owed my august position neither to a natural taste for feminine affairs, nor to earnest and sustained industry, nor to precocity. My original situation, as assistant editor of the paper, had not been unconnected with a purchase of debentures; and I succeeded, after a very few years, to the editorship simply because the editor wished to retire and there was no one else handy to take his place. Merit or talent had little or nothing to do with my sensational rise in the world.

When I think of my editorial staff and my regular contributors (writers and artists) tears come into my eyes, as they would sometimes come into the eyes of those women for whom my smile was sunshine and my frown (so rare) rain and sleet and snow. They were all young, those ladies, but it never occurred to me that they were young. I deemed every one of them middle-aged, like myself. Without exception they were devoted to duty;

and their loyalty to the welfare of the paper could not be disputed. I believe, too, that they had knowledge of their subjects – frocks, cloaks, lingerie, boots, gloves, shops, bargains, food, cookery, housekeeping, children, hygiene, smart society.

But I regret to say that they had defects. The artists could not draw. Nothing surprising in that. Fashion artists were not supposed to be able to draw. They were supposed to know by heart the curves of a certain stock figure and to reproduce the said figure in the only two attitudes permitted by the existing cast-iron traditions of journalism for ladies – standing and seated. The figures were invariably portrayed either solitary or in a universe peopled solely by women. No male figures ever appeared in a fashion sketch. The figures were all taller than life and slimmer than life, with hands and fingers longer than life; and they all wore their lips sweetly parted in an everlasting simper. It was held proper for them to look brainless and silly, and they always did look brainless and silly. I cared not; I was not troubled by the extraordinary unlikeness of the figures to any human being created by heaven.

What did trouble me was that the writers did not know how to write, and I was passionately interested in the art of writing. I had very clear notions about literary style. My contributors knew naught about literary style; they had never heard of literary style. True, they had heard of grammar, but not one of them understood the principles of grammar. When I pointed out to them that the first business of a journalist is to write, and that in journalism knowledge and tastes are useless until they are set down on paper clearly and neatly in a manner agreeable to read and easy to understand, the young ladies were thunderstruck. In the worst crises of work I would try to teach them grammar, but without any marked success. Occasionally they would weep – not because of my brutality, but because of their own unworthiness. I could tolerate anything but tears. When they cried, I would beg of them to leave the presence.

Once an unknown girl sent in an unsolicited contribution which was faultlessly grammatical and which I could read, if not with delight, without positive pain. I invited this bird of paradise to visit me, and I engaged her at a salary on the spot. Things improved.

Woman was supposed to be, and was, an "advanced" paper. Its motto, printed on the first page of every number, was "Forward but not too fast". Owing to the looseness and vagueness of the English language, this phrase could unhappily be interpreted in two very different meanings, and the ribald missed few opportunities of jeering at it. Nevertheless, it did plainly indicate an editorial belief that the status and activities of women ought to be raised and enlarged.

So far so good. But we were so determined to offend the feelings of nobody that our columns almost never indicated in what direction feminine progress ought to be made. No downright opinion upon any really controversial topic affecting the relations of the sexes was ever expressed. "Safety First" is supposed to be quite a new slogan. It is not new. It was ever the private watchword of editors; it was ours; it is the watchword of all editors today, and it will be the watchword of all editors tomorrow and eternally.

Nevertheless, *Woman* did mysteriously acquire a reputation for being in the van of progressive movements, though nobody who now examined its files could possibly conceive why. It had also the reputation of being the most intellectual woman's magazine in existence. It may have been. But, if so, what must the others have been like!

Its aim was certainly to satisfy the tastes of educated women, or women who wanted to be educated – and not to go beyond those interests. Hence, naturally, politics were excluded from its pages. A woman's politics were those of her husband, if she had one; and those of her male relatives if she was unmarried. If she had neither husband nor male relative then she had no politics, as to which her mind, assuming she was right minded and not an abandoned female, was a white blank.

The make-up of the paper was calculated to give the impression that the chief interest of educated women was the doings of exalted social circles, for these were always allotted the first place. The impression was not in accordance with facts; by which I mean that it was false. The genuine editorial conviction was that the chief interest of educated woman was her personal appearance, and articles and news and drawings intended to help her to make the very best of her personal appearance constituted the main part of the paper.

Only there was supposed to be something not quite avowable in this chief interest. There was a suspicion that an educated woman ought to have a soul above solicitude for her personal appearance, and accordingly the dress-and-looks department was not flaunted on the forehead of the paper. The day had not arrived when a perfect lady of education and taste could, by taking out her mirror and rouging and powdering herself in the middle of a banquet, with a man on either side of her, publish shameless to the world that personal appearance was her continual pre-occupation and that she didn't care who saw how much of it was faked and how much was heaven-made.

Indeed, though paint and powder were by no means unknown or unemployed, a convention prevailed that they were not employed, and further that truly nice women would not employ them. To destroy the character of a woman you had only to call her "painted". Assuredly, within my recollection, *Woman* never advocated nor offered advice about either paint or powder, and I can remember no advertisements of such. It was all very touching.

Next after personal appearance came housekeeping, furnishing, and health or hygiene. The first two were dedicated to the universal and eternal feminine desire to obtain half-a-crown's worth of stuff for two shillings; and nothing more need be said about them. As for health and hygiene, they had to be handled with the finest delicacy, and they were. An example: I recall remarking to a circle of regular contributors that corsets as then worn were unhealthy, unhygienic, and indefensible. Nobody could honestly deny the truth of the statement, but if I had asserted that the Ten Commandments were indefensible I could not have produced a greater horror on sweet earnest countenances. I was made to understand that if my opinion got about, if the slightest hint of it escaped, the paper would be utterly ruined. Therefore my opinion was not permitted to get about. So much for health and hygiene.

Literature and the arts were not neglected in the progressive organ. Having very strong feelings about them, I attended to them personally and in my own way. My articles on new books were of so advanced a kind that they might, as effectually as my unorthodox views on corsets, have ruined the paper – had they been read. Similarly with criticisms of the drama. Occasionally

I wrote on picture exhibitions, and on concerts in the same strain. (I had various pseudonyms.) There was no hand to prevent me, because I was the editor; and I feel sure that no paper for educated ladies had ever before published such manifestoes on literature and the arts.

These contributions undoubtedly worked ill to the periodical either negatively or positively. If read, all the readers, save a very few, must have considered them odd, not nice, or simply dangerous. But they were not read.

Nor do I think that my Paris dress correspondence (which I wrote weekly in Fetter Lane after perusing French dailies bought in Coventry Street) was read – at any rate deliberately. In those days the majority of women did not in fact bother their heads about Paris fashions. Paris was a name and nothing more . . .

The Potteries: A Sketch

In August 1897 Tertia Bennett's fiancé was drowned. Bennett went up to the Potteries to see her, and on 10 September he wrote in his *Journal*: "During this week, when I have been taking early morning walks with Tertia, and when I have been traversing the district after dark, the grim and original beauty of certain aspects of the Potteries, to which I have referred in the introduction to *Anna Tellwright* (*Anna of the Five Towns*), has fully revealed itself to me for the first time . . ." The following article was the immediate consequence. It was published in *Black and White* on 12 March 1898. Bennett doubtless revised *Anna of the Five Towns* in the light of his experience: the novel was in composition from September 1896 to May 1901.

❧   ❧   ❧

North of a line drawn from the Wash to the beak of Carnarvon, and due south of the Trent's source, lies a tract of country some seven miles long by four at its widest, bearing in shape a rough similarity to the contour of England, less Cornwall and Devon. Its face is an unbroken alternation of hillock and valley, the highest hills scarcely reaching 300 feet, and in the whole of it there is no river broader than a brook.

This is the home of pottery. Five contiguous towns, whose red-brown bricks have inundated the moorland like a succession of great lakes strung together by some St Lawrence of a main road, devote themselves, with several smaller townships, to the manufacture from their own and other clays of every sort of earthenware, china and porcelain. In these parts the sound of the shattering of an earthen vessel, elsewhere unpleasing to the housewife's ear, is music; for upon the frequency of such fractures all the world over the welfare, almost the very existence, of the inhabitants chiefly depends. The towns are mean and ugly in appearance – sombre, shapeless, hard-featured, uncouth; and the vaporous poison of their ovens and chimneys has soiled and shrivelled the surrounding greenness of Nature till there is no country lane within miles but what presents a gaunt travesty of rural charms. Nothing could be more prosaic than the aspect of the huddled streets; nothing more seemingly remote from romance. Yet romance dwells even here, though unsuspected by its very makers – the romance which always attends the alchemic processes of skilled, transmuting labour. The infrequent poet may yield himself to its influence as, wandering on the scarred heights above the densest of the smoke-wrack, he suddenly comprehends the secret significance of the vast, effective Doing which here continually goes forward; the stranger who is being conducted through some "works" may vaguely divine a miracle while he watches the slow transformations of the tortured clay from the pug-mill to the long room, where, amid chatter and clatter, young girls smooth the finished ware with knives; the dreaming native may get a nameless thrill when in an unfamiliar street the low thunder of subterranean machinery or a glimpse of the creative craftsman through a dark window startles his sleepy senses. But these appreciations are exceptional enough to prove the main fact that the nimbus of romance beautifying the squalor, softening the coarseness of all this indispensable work, shines unperceived.

Because they seldom think, the townsmen take shame when indicted for having disfigured half a county in order to live. They do not see that this disfigurement is just an incident in the unending warfare of man and Nature, and calls for no contrition. Here, indeed, is Nature repaid for some of her notorious cruelties. She imperiously bids man sustain and reproduce himself, and this is one of the places where in the act itself of obedience he insults and horribly maltreats her. To go out beyond the municipal confines where, in the thick of the altercation, the subsidiary industries of coal and iron prosper amid a wreck of verdure, ought surely to raise one's estimate not only of man but of Nature: so thorough and ruthless is his havoc of her, and so indomitable her ceaseless recuperation. The struggle is grim, tremendous, heroic; on the one side a wresting from Nature's own bowels of the means to waste her; on the other an undismayed, enduring fortitude, with now and then a smart return blow in the shape of a mine-explosion or a famine. And if here man has made of the very daylight an infamy, he can boast that he adds to the darkest night the weird beauty of fire, and flame-tinted cloud. From roof and hill you may see on every side furnace calling to furnace with fiery tongues and wreathing messages of smoke across the blue-red glow of acres of burning ironstone. The unique pyrotechnics of labour atoning for its grime!

This race of contemners of Nature bears the inevitable characteristics of its environment. It is harsh in dialect, religion, and sport; indifferent to visible loveliness, but delighting in the beauty of sound, especially the sound of brass bands and human song, and singing naturally – like the Elizabethans; cunning ("No people whatever are esteemed more subtle," said Plott, in the seventeenth century); striving and scornful of the languid South; thriving in spite of those deep-rooted intestinal jealousies which for a thousand years hindered any advance upon a system of local government invented by Alfred. But what stands out most saliently is the ancient instinctive sympathy – at once the fruit and the one monument of immemorial tradition – which the people have for their craft. Even in the mother-town, whose borders have yielded clay to the potter since before the beginning of history, there is no palpable trace of an unrivalled antiquity, unless it be a squat church tower, black and grey with eight centuries of smoke. The past lives solely, and lives perhaps sufficiently, in that exquisite accord between workman and work which everywhere manifests itself and which only the longest use could have so perfected.

In Watling Street

Bennett went to live at Trinity Hall Farm, near Hockliffe, Bedfordshire, in October 1900, and he brought his parents to live with him. Along with a few other books, he wrote *Teresa of Watling Street* there, a work which he described to E. V. Lucas many years afterwards as "the world's worst novel". The following essay was published in the *English Review* in September 1911, and reprinted in *Paris Nights* in 1913.

🙥 🙥 🙥

Upon an evening in early autumn, I, who had never owned an orchard before, stood in my orchard; behind me were a phalanx of some sixty trees bearing (miraculously, to my simplicity) a fine crop of apples and plums – my apples and plums, and a mead of some two acres, my mead, upon which I discerned possibilities of football and cricket; behind these was a double greenhouse containing three hundred pendent bunches of grapes of the dark and aristocratic variety which I thought I had seen in Piccadilly ticketed at four shillings a pound – my grapes; still further behind uprose the chimneys of a country-house, uncompromisingly plain and to some eyes perhaps ugly, but my country-house, the lease of which, stamped, was in my pocket. Immediately in front of me was a luxuriant hedge which, long unclipped, had attained a height of at least fifteen feet. Beyond the hedge the ground fell away sharply into a draining ditch, and on the other side of the ditch, through the interstices of the hedge, I perceived glimpses of a very straight and very white highway.

This highway was Watling Street, built of the Romans, and even now surviving as the most famous road in England. I had "learnt" it at school, and knew that it once ran from Dover to London, from London to Chester and from Chester to York. Just recently I had tracked it diligently on a series of county maps, and discovered that, though only vague fragments of it remained in Kent, Surrey, Shropshire, Cheshire, and Yorkshire, it still flourished and abounded exceedingly in my particular neighbourhood as a right line, austere, renowned, indispensable, clothed in its own immortal dust. I could see but patches of it in the twilight, but I was aware that it stretched fifteen miles southeast of me, and unnumbered miles northwest of me, with scarcely a curve to break the splendid inexorable monotony of its career. To me it was a wonderful road – more wonderful than the Great North Road, or the military road from Moscow to Vladivostok. And the most wonderful thing about it was that I lived on it. After all, few people can stamp the top of their notepaper, "Watling Street, England". It is not a residential thoroughfare.

Only persons of imagination can enter into my feelings at that moment. I had spent two-thirds of my life in a town (squalid, industrial) and the remaining third in Town. I thought I knew every creosoted block in Fleet Street, every bookstall in Shoreditch, every hosier's in Piccadilly. I certainly did know the order of stations on the Inner Circle, the various frowns of publishers, the strange hysteric, silly atmosphere of theatrical first-nights, and stars of the Empire and Alhambra (by sight), and the vicious odours of a thousand and one restaurants. And lo! burdened with all this accumulated knowledge, shackled by all these habits, associations, entrancements, I was yet moved by some mysterious and far-off atavism to pack up, harness the oxen, "trek", and go and live in "the country".

Of course I soon discovered that there is no such thing as "the country", just as there is no such thing as Herbert Spencer's "state". "The country" is an entity which exists only in the brains of an urban population, whose members ridiculously regard the terrene surface as a concatenation of towns surrounded by earthy space. There is England, and there are spots on England called towns: that is all. But at that time I too had the illusion of "the country", a district where one saw "trees", "flowers", and "birds". For me, a tree was not an oak or an ash or an elm or a birch or a chestnut; it was just a "tree". For me there were robins, sparrows, and crows; the rest of the winged fauna was merely "birds". I recognised roses, daisies, dandelions, forget-me-nots, chrysanthemums, and one or two more blossoms; all else was "flowers". Remember that all this happened before the advent of the nature-book and the sublime invention of week-ending, and conceive me plunging into this unknown, inscrutable and recondite "country", as I might have plunged fully clothed and unable to swim into the sea. It was a prodigious adventure! When my friends asked me, with furtive glances at each other as in the presence of a lunatic, why I was going to live in the country, I could only reply: "Because I want to. I want to see what it's like." I might have attributed my action to the dearness of season-tickets on the Underground, to the slowness of omnibuses or the danger of cabs: my friends would have been just as wise, and I just as foolish, in their esteem. I admit that their attitude of benevolent contempt, of far-seeing sagacity, gave me to think. And although I was obstinate, it was with a pang of misgiving that I posted the notice of quitting my suburban residence; and the pang was more acute when I signed the contract for the removal of my furniture. I called on my friends before the sinister day of exodus.

"Good-bye," I said.

"Au revoir," they replied, with calm vaticinatory assurance, "we shall see you back again in a year."

❖   ❖   ❖

Thus, outwardly braggart, inwardly quaking, I departed. The quaking had not ceased as I stood, in the autumn twilight, in my beautiful orchard, in front of my country-house. Toiling up the slope from the southward, I saw an enormous van with three horses: the last instalment of my chattels. As it turned lumberingly at right angles into my private road or boreen, I said aloud:

"I've done it."

I had. I felt like a statesman who has handed an ultimatum to a king's messenger. No withdrawal was now possible. From the reverie natural to this melancholy occasion I was aroused by a disconcerting sound of collision, the rattle of chains, and the oaths customary to drivers in a difficulty. I ran towards the house and down the weedy drive bordered by trees which a learned gardener had told me were of the variety *cupressus lawsoniana*. In essaying the perilous manoeuvre of twisting round three horses and a long van on a space about twenty feet square, the driver had overset the brick pier upon which swung my garden-gate. The unicorn horse of the team was nosing at the *cupressus lawsoniana* and the van was scotched in the gateway. I thought, "This is an omen." I was, however, reassured by the sight of two butchers and two bakers each asseverating that nothing could afford him greater pleasure than to call every day for orders. A minute later the postman, in his own lordly equipage, arrived with my newspapers and his respects. I tore open a paper and read news of London. I convinced myself that London actually existed, though I were never to see it again. The smashing of the pier dwindled from a catastrophe to an episode.

❖   ❖   ❖

The next morning very early I was in Watling Street. Since then

> Full many a glorious morning have I seen
> Flatter the mountain tops with sovereign eye,

but this was the first in the sequence of those Shakespearean mornings, and it was also, subjectively, the finest. I shall not describe it, since, objectively and in the quietude of hard fact, I now perceive that it could not have been in the least remarkable. The sun rose over the southward range which Bunyan took for the model of his Delectable Mountains, and forty or fifty square miles of diversified land was spread out in front of me. The road cut down for a couple of miles like a geometrician's rule, and disappeared in a slight S curve, the work of a modern generation afraid of gradients, on to the other side of the Delectable Mountains. I thought: "How magnificent were those Romans in their disregard of everything except direction!" And being a pro-

fessional novelist I naturally began at once to consider the possibilities of exploiting Watling Street in fiction. Then I climbed to
the brow of my own hill, whence, at the foot of the long northerly
slope, I could descry the outposts of my village, a mile away;
there was no habitation of mankind nearer to me than this picturesque and venerable hamlet, which seemed to lie inconsiderable
on the great road like a piece of paper. The seventy-four telegraph
wires which border the great road run above the roofs of Winghurst as if they were unaware of its existence. "And Winghurst,"
I reflected, "is henceforth my metropolis." No office! No memor-
ising of time-tables! No daily struggle-for-lunch! Winghurst,
with three hundred inhabitants, the centre of excitement, the fount
of external life!

The course of these ordinary but inevitable thoughts was inter-
rupted by my consciousness of a presence near me. A man
coughed. He had approached me, in almost soleless boots, on the
grassy footpath. For a brief second I regarded him with that peculiar fellow-feeling which a man who has risen extremely early is
wont to exhibit towards another man who has risen extremely
early. But finding no answering vanity in his undistinguished
features I quickly put on an appearance of usualness, to indicate
that I might be found on that spot at that hour every morning.
The man looked shabby, and that Sherlock Holmes who lies
concealed in each one of us decided for me that he must be a tailor
out-of-work.

"Good morning, sir," he said.

"Good morning," I said.

"Do you want to buy a good recipe for a horse, sir?" he asked.

"A horse?" I repeated, wondering whether he was a lunatic, or
a genius who had discovered a way to manufacture horses.

"Yes, sir," he said, "They often fall sick, sir, you know. The
saying is, as I daresay you've heard, 'Never trust a woman's word
or a horse's health.' "

I corrected his quotation.

"I've got one or two real good recipes," he resumed.

"But I've got no horse," I replied, and that seemed to finish the
interview.

"No offence, I hope, sir," he said, and passed on towards the
Delectable Mountains.

44

He was a mystery; his speech disclosed no marked local accent; he had certainly had some education; and he was hawking horse-remedies in Watling Street at sunrise. Here was the germ of my first lesson in rusticity. Except in towns, the "horsey" man does not necessarily look horsey. That particular man resembled a tailor, and by a curious coincidence the man most fearfully and wonderfully learned in equine lore that I have yet known is a tailor.

But horses! Six miles away to the West I could see the steam of expresses on the London and North Western Main line; four miles to the East I could see the steam of expresses on the Midland. And here was an individual offering stable-recipes as simply as though they had been muffins! I reflected on my empty stable, harness-room, coach-house. I began to suspect that I was in a land where horses entered in the daily and hourly existence of the people. I had known for weeks that I must buy a horse; the nearest town and the nearest railway station were three miles off. But now, with apprehension, I saw that mysterious and dangerous mercantile operation to be dreadfully imminent: me, *coram publico,* buying a horse, me the dupe of copers, me a butt for the covert sarcasm of a village omniscient about horses and intolerant of ignorance on such a subject!

✦   ✦   ✦

Down in the village, that early morning, I saw a pony and an evidently precarious trap standing in front of the principal shop. I had read about the "village-shop" in novels; I had even ventured to describe it in fiction of my own; and I was equally surprised and delighted to find that the village-shop of fiction was also the village-shop of fact. It was the mere truth that one could buy everything in this diminutive emporium, that the multifariousness of its odours excelled that of the odours of Cologne, and that the proprietor, who had never seen me before, instantly knew me and all about me. Soon I was in a fair way to know something of the proprietor. He was informing me that he had five little children, when one of the five, snuffling and in a critical mood, tumbled into the shop out of an obscure Beyond.

"And what's your name?" I enquired of the girl, with that

fatuous, false blandness of tone which the inexpert always adopt towards children. I thought of the five maidens whose names were five sweet symphonies, and moreover I deemed it politic to establish friendly relations with my monopolist.

"She's a little shy," I remarked.

"It's a boy, sir," said the monopolist.

It occurred to me that Nature was singularly uninventive in devising new quandaries for the foolish.

"Tell the gentleman your name."

Thus admonished, the boy emitted one monosyllable: "Guy."

"We called him Guy because he was born on the fifth of November," the monopolist was good enough to explain.

As I left the shop a man driving a pony drew up at the door with an immense and sudden flourish calculated to impress the simple. I noticed that the pony was the same animal which I had previously seen standing there.

"Want to buy a pony, sir?" The question was thrown at me like a missile that narrowly escaped my head; launched in a voice which must once have been extremely powerful, but which now, whether by abuse of shouting in the open air or by the deteriorating effect of gin on the vocal chords, was only a loud, passionate whisper: so that, though the man obviously bawled with all his might, the drum of one's ear was not shattered. I judged, partly from the cut of his coat and the size of the buttons on it, and partly from the creaminess of the shaggy, long-tailed pony, that my questioner was or had been connected with circuses. His very hand was against him; the turned-back podgy thumb showed acquisitiveness, and the enormous Gophir diamonds in brass rings argued a certain lack of really fine taste. His face had literally the brazen look, and that absolutely hard, impudent, glaring impassivity acquired only by those who earn more than enough to drink by continually bouncing the public.

"The finest pony in the county, sir." (It was an animal organism gingerly supported on four crooked legs; a quadruped and nothing more.) "The finest pony in the county!" he screamed, "Finest pony in England, sir! Not another like him! I took him to the Rothschild horse-show, but they wouldn't have him. Said I'd come too late to enter him for the first-clawss. They were afraid – afferaid! There was the water-jump. 'Stand aside, you blighters,'

I said, 'and he'll jump that, the d – – d gig and all.' But they were afferaid!"

I asked if the animal was quiet to drive.

"Quiet to drive, sir, did you say? I should *say* so. I says *Away*, and *off* he goes." Here the thin scream became a screech. "Then I says *Pull up, you blighter*, and he stops dead. A child could drive him. He don't want no driving. You could drive him with a silken thread." His voice melted and with an exquisite tender cadence he repeated: "With a silk-en therredd!"

"Well," I said. "How much?"

"How much, did you say, sir? How much?" He made it appear that this question came upon him as an extraordinary surprise. I nodded.

He meditated on the startling problem, and then yelled: "Thirty guineas. It's giving him away."

"Make it shillings," I said. I was ingenuously satisfied with my retort, but the man somehow failed to appreciate it.

"Come here," he said, in a tone of intimate confidence. "Come here. Listen. I've had that pony's picture painted. Finest artist in England, sir. And frame! You never see such a frame! At thirty guineas I'll throw the picture in. Look ye! That picture cost me two quid, and here's the receipt." He pulled forth a grimy paper, and I accepted it from his villainous fingers. It proved, however, to be a receipt for four pounds, and for the portrait, not of a pony, but of a man.

"This is a receipt for your own portrait," I said.

"Now wasn't that a coorious mistake for me to make?" he asked, as if demanding information. "Wasn't that a coorious mistake?"

I was obliged to give him the answer he desired, and then he produced the correct receipt.

"Now," he said wooingly. "There! Is it a trade? I'll bring you the picture to-night. Finest frame you ever saw! What? No? Look here, buy him at thirty guineas – say pounds – and I'll chuck you both the blighted pictures in!"

"*Away!*" he screamed a minute later, and the cream pony, galvanised into frantic activity by that sound, and surely not controllable by a silken thread, scurried off towards the Delectable Mountains.

This was my first insight into horse dealing.

France

In the years from 1898 to 1902 Bennett made an impressive advance on several fronts: he established himself in the *Academy* as one of the liveliest critics of the day; he made a splash in light serial fiction with *The Grand Babylon Hotel* (1901–2) and in light essays with his "Savoir-Faire Papers" in *T.P.'s Weekly* (beginning in November 1902); and he pleased the highbrow literary world with *Anna of the Five Towns* (1902). The prospects were sufficiently bright for him to be able to give up editing *Woman* in September 1900. With his father's death in 1902 and his mother's subsequent return to the Five Towns, he was free to live and work where he chose. He gave up Trinity Hall Farm in January 1903, travelled in Algeria for a month or more, returned to England briefly, and on 15 March went to France. He lived for several weeks at the Hôtel du quai Voltaire, returned to England for several weeks, and then took a flat at 4 rue de Calais, where he stayed until the end of 1906.

The following two pieces are the first sections of "My Reminiscences", which was published in the *Strand Magazine* in February 1913 and a month earlier in the *Metropolitan Magazine* in America. It was reprinted in *Things That Have Interested Me* in 1921.

The Desire for France

When one looks back one sees that certain threads run through one's life, making a sort of pattern in it. These threads and the nature of the pattern are not perceived until long after the actual events constituting them. I now see that there has been a French thread through my life. Of its origin I can form no idea, for neither my forbears nor the friends of my youth displayed the slightest interest in France or the French. Yet when I was eighteen or nineteen, and a clerk in my father's law office in the Five Towns, I used to spend my money on French novels – in English translations. I was obliged to be content with English translations because I could not read French without a dictionary, a book of idioms, and intense weariness. I had been studying French almost daily for nine years. I had passed the London Matriculation in French – and let me say that the London Matriculation French paper is, or was, among the silliest and most futile absurdities that the perverse, unimaginative craftiness of the pedagogic mind ever invented. I knew an immense amount of French grammar. And all my labour was, in practice, utterly useless. In such wise are living languages taught on this island. Nevertheless, I deeply enjoyed these secret contacts with French thought and manners, as revealed in French novels. The risks I had to run in order to procure them were terrific. Talk about leading a double life under the paternal roof! I had no need to inquire whether modern French novels would be permitted at home. I very well knew that they would not. Victor Hugo alone would have been permitted, and him I had already gulped down in three huge doses. Still my father was a very broad-minded man for his epoch and situation. But there are limits – anyhow, in the Five Towns.

I used to order these perilous works from a bookseller who was not the official family bookseller; and I used to say to him, as casually as I could: "Don't send it up; I'll call for it." One Saturday afternoon I reached home earlier than my father. This was a wonder, for it was no part of my business to leave the office before the head thereof. I was supposed to remain at the office until he had thought fit to go, and then to follow him at a decent interval. However, on that day I preceded him. Going into the dining-room, I saw on the corner of the sideboard nearest the door – exactly where my father's parcels and letters were put to await him – a translation of a novel by Paul Bourget which I had ordered. I have never been more startled than I was in that instant. The mere thought of the danger I was courting overwhelmed me. I snatched the volume and ran upstairs with it; it might have been a bomb of which the fuse was lighted. At the same moment I heard on the glass panel of the front door the peculiar metallic rap which my father made with his ring finger. (He would never carry a latchkey.) Heaven had deigned to save me! Distinguished as Paul Bourget is, respectable as he is, there would have been an enormous and disastrous shindy over his novel had my father seen it. Whether the bookseller had sinned through carelessness or whether, suspecting that I was ultimately bound for the inferno of Paris, he had basely hoped to betray me to my father, I do not know. But I think the kindest thing I can, though to send forth a French novel without concealing it in brown paper was perfectly inexcusable at that period in the Five Towns.

❖ ❖ ❖

Later I seemed to lose interest in French literature. It was not until I had been in London for a year or two that I turned towards it again. I remember making the delightful discovery that a French novel could, after all, be read in the original without a dictionary, provided one was content with a somewhat vague idea of the sense. The first French book I ever read in this way was Daudet's *Fromont Jeune et Risler Aîné*. I was then about twenty-three or twenty-four. Thenceforward I never ceased to read French, and, by a well-known mental process, I was continually learning the meaning of new words and phrases without consulting the dictionary. I used to buy a French newspaper nearly every day at a shop in Coventry Street. What I made of it all I cannot now conceive. Gradually the legend grew up around me that I was an authority on French literature, and when I became a reviewer French books were very frequently sent to me for criticism, because of my alleged special competence. I would go to French plays in London. When indiscreet persons demanded, "But do you understand?" I would reply, "Not all, of course." It was the truth; I did not understand all. It was also in essence a dreadful lie, for I understood nothing.

❖   ❖   ❖

Strange detail: I began to take private lessons in German (in which language also I had satisfied the University of London). I chose German because I thought I knew enough French! Another strange detail: I used often to say to my friends, "As soon as I am free enough I shall go and live in Paris." And yet I had no hope whatever of being able to go to Paris as a resident. I doubt if I had any genuine intention of going. But it was my habit to make such idle forecasts and boasts; seemingly they convinced everybody but me. I think now that something subconscious must have prompted them. They have all been justified by events. Chance, of course, has aided. Thus, from about the age of twenty-five onwards I used to say: "I shall marry at forty." I had absolutely no ground of personal conviction for this prophecy. But, by a sheer accident, I did happen to marry at forty. And everyone, impressed, went about remarking, "He always does what he says he'll do."

❖   ❖   ❖

Similarly, I did go to live in Paris. A remarkable group of circumstances left me free from all local ties to earn my living where I chose. I was then thirty-five. Did I fly straight to Paris? Not a bit. I could not decide what to do. I went to Algeria first. On my way home I lingered in Paris. I question if I was very powerfully drawn towards Paris at the moment. I had to come to England to fulfil a social engagement, and then I returned to Paris for a few days, with the notion of establishing myself at Tours for a year or two, to "perfect" my French. I remained in Paris for five years, and in France for over nine years, liking and comprehending the French more and more, and feeling more and more at home among them, until now I do believe I have a kind of double mentality – one English and the other French. Naturally, when I settled in Paris, all my friends said again, "He always said he would do it, and he has done it." My reputation as a man of his word was made indestructible. But to me the affair presents itself as chiefly accidental.

❖   ❖   ❖

I had awful difficulties with the language. Somehow, very illogically, I thought that the mere fact of residence in Paris would mysteriously increase my knowledge of the French tongue to a respectable degree. I remember I was advised to haunt the theatre if I wished to "perfect" my French. The first play I saw was Edmond Sée's *L'Indiscret* at the Théâtre Antoine. I entered the theatre hoping for the best. I had read the play in advance. I did not, however, succeed in comprehending one single word – not one. I had been studying French for nearly twenty-six years. The man in me who had written scores of "authoritative" articles on French literature was deeply humiliated. I at once arranged to take lessons. Three or four nights a week I was to be seen in the first row of the stalls (so as to hear well) of the little *théâtres de quartier* round about Montmarte. I seemed to make no progress for six months. Then, enchantingly, I began to understand bits of phrases heard in the street. I had turned the corner! Heavenly moment!

Paris Flats

The world revolves very rapidly under its appearance of stability. Only yesterday it seems that I was settling in Paris. And yet then I could buy Empire chairs (*croisées*) at sixteen shillings apiece; I could buy an Empire bedstead for a couple of pounds; and a beautiful dressing-table, whose mirror was supported by the curved necks of the Imperial swans, for three pounds! If I went to Paris now and asked dealers for Empire furniture at such prices I should be classed as a lunatic. I had lived in an hotel overlooking the Seine for some time, and I was taking possession of a flat and furnishing it. I chose the Empire style for the furniture because I wanted a French style, and the Empire style was the only style within the means of a man who had to earn his living by realistic fiction. Louis Quinze and Louis Seize are not for writers; neither is Empire, any more! To acquire some real comprehension of a nation's character it is necessary to fit out a home in its capital. The process brings you at once into direct contact with the very spirit of the race. Especially in the big shops, which are so racy a feature of Paris life, do you encounter the French spirit, traditions, and idiosyncrasy. At some of the big shops you can buy every-thing that makes a home – except of course the second-hand. But you must not traverse the immemorial customs of home-making in France. Try to depart from the rule, even as to servants' aprons, and you will soon see that mysterious powers and influences are arrayed against you. The Republic itself stands before you in the shape of the shop-assistant. France is a land of suave uniformity. It is also at once the paradise and the inferno of bureaucracy. There the bureaucracy is underworked and underpaid. All which has been said before, uncountably often. Every Englishman is aware of it. And yet no Englishman is truly aware of it who has not set up a home in France.

◇   ◇   ◇

For example, I wanted the gas to be turned on in my flat. A simple affair! Drop a post card to the Company telling the Company to come and turn it on? Not at all! I was told that it would be better to call upon the Company. So I called.

"What do you desire, monsieur?"

"I am the new tenant of a flat, and I want the gas turned on."

"Ah! You are the new tenant of a flat, and you want the gas turned on. M. Chose, here is the new tenant of a flat, and he wants the gas turned on. Where should he be led to?"

About a quarter of an hour of this, and then at last I am led by a municipal employé, sure of his job and of his pension, to the far-distant rooms of the higher employé appointed by the City of Paris to deal with such as me. This room is furnished somewhat like that of a solicitor's managing clerk.

"Good morning, sir."

"Good morning, sir."

"It appears, sir – M. Bennay, fourth floor, No. 4 Rue de Calais, sixth arrondissement, is it not? – that you want the gas turned on. Will you put yourself to the trouble of sitting down, M. Bennay?"

I sit down. He sits down.

"Ah! So you want the gas turned on! Let us see, let us see – "

Hundreds of such applications must be made every day. But the attitude of this ceremonious official might be put into words thus: "A strange and interesting application of yours – to have the gas turned on! Very remarkable! It attracts me. The case must be examined with the care and respect which it deserves."

The next moment the official astonishingly rises and informs me that the papers will arrive in due course. I depart. The papers do arrive in due course, papers of all colours and all complexities. One or two tips, and I get the gas. Electricity was not so easy. The Treaty of Berlin did not demand more negotiations and diplomacy than my electricity.

◇ ◇ ◇

On the other hand, I had no trouble with the police. Every foreign resident must report himself to the police and get a permit to exist. The machine for preventing the unwelcome from existing in France is a beautiful bit of engineering. I ignored the police and just went on existing. Nothing happened. Yet sundry men must have been bringing up families and providing dowries for their daughters on salaries which they received for duties which included looking after me.

I said that it was necessary to fit out a home in a country in order to comprehend the national character. Perhaps that is not enough. You must get married in that country. Let none say that he knows his Paris until he has persuaded the mayor of some arrondissement to unite him in matrimony to a woman. By the time the ceremony is over, and the certificate issued, he will be a genuine expert in the niceties of the French temperament.

Artistic Evening

The following essay presumably concerns an evening
in the spring or autumn of 1903. Very likely it is composed of several evenings and presented with certain
disguises in the identities of host and other guests.
Among Bennett's closest friends in Paris at the time
were Henry Davray, editor and translator (1873–
1944), and Marcel Schwob, the author (1867–1905),
to whom Bennett dedicated *Tales of the Five Towns* in
1905. The essay was published in the *English Review*
in November 1910, and reprinted in *Paris Nights*.

ꞔ꙼ ꞔ꙼ ꞔ꙼

The first invitation I ever received into a purely Parisian interior
might have been copied out of a novel by Paul Bourget. Its lure
was thus phrased: "Un peu de musique et d'agréables femmes".
It answered to my inward vision of Paris. My experiences in
London, which fifteen years earlier I had entered with my mouth
open as I might have entered some city of Oriental romance, had,
of course, done little to destroy my illusions about Paris, for the
ingenuousness of the artist is happily indestructible. Hence, my
inward vision of Paris was romantic, based on the belief that
Paris was essentially "different". Nothing more banal in London
than a "little music", or even "some agreeable women"! But
what a difference between a little music and *un peu de musique*!
What an exciting difference between agreeable women and

55

agréables femmes! After all, this difference remains nearly intact to this day. Nobody who has not lived intimately in and with Paris can appreciate the unique savour of that word *femmes*. "Women" is a fine word, a word which, breathed in a certain tone, will make all men – even bishops, misogynists and political propagandists – fall to dreaming! But *femmes* is yet more potent. There cling to it the associations of a thousand years of dalliance in a land where dalliance is passionately understood.

The usual Paris flat, high up, like the top drawer of a chest of drawers! No passages, but multitudinous doors. In order to arrive at any given room it is necessary to pass through all the others. I passed through the dining-room, where a servant with a marked geometrical gift had arranged a number of very small plates round the rim of a vast circular table. In the drawing-room my host was seated at a grand piano with a couple of candles in front of him and a couple of women behind him. See the light glinting on bits of the ebon piano, and on his face, and on their chins and jewels, and on the corner of a distant picture frame; and all the rest of the room obscure! He wore a jacket, negligently; the interest of his attire was dramatically centred in his large, limp necktie; necktie such as none but a hero could unfurl in London. A man with a very intelligent face, eager, melancholy (with a sadness acquired in the Divorce Court), wistful, appealing. An idealist! He called himself a publicist. One of the women, a musical composer, had a black skirt and a white blouse; she was ugly but provocative. The other, all in white, was pretty and sprightly, but her charm lacked the perverseness which is expected and usually found in Paris; she painted, she versified, she recited. With the eye of a man who had sat for years in the editorial chair of a ladies' paper, I looked instinctively at the hang of the skirts. It was not good. Those vague frocks were such as had previously been something else, and would soon be transformed by discreet modifications into something still else. Candlelight was best for them. But what grace of demeanour, what naturalness, what candid ease and appositeness of greeting, what absence of self-consciousness! Paris is the self-unconscious.

I was presented as *le romancier anglais*. It sounded romantic. I thought: "What a false impression they are getting, as of some vocation exotic and delightful! If only they knew the prose of it!"

I thought of their conception of England, a mysterious isle. When Balzac desired to make a woman exquisitely strange, he caused her to be born in Lancashire.

My host begged permission to go on playing. In the intervals of being a publicist, he composed music, and he was now deciphering a manuscript freshly written. I bent over between the two women and read the title:

"Ygdrasil: rêverie."

❖   ❖   ❖

When there were a dozen or fifteen people in the room, and as many candles irregularly disposed like lighthouses over a complex archipelago, I formed one of a group consisting of those two women and another, a young dramatist who concealed his expressive hands in a pair of bright yellow gloves, and a middle-aged man whose constitution was obviously ruined. This last was librarian of some public library – I forget which – and was stated to be monstrously erudite in all literatures. I asked him whether he had of late encountered anything new and good in English.

"I have read nothing later than Swinburne", he replied in a thin, pinched voice – like his features, like his wary and suffering eyes. Speaking with an icy, glittering pessimism, he quoted Stendhal to the effect that a man does not change after twenty-five. He supported the theory bitterly and joyously, and seemed to taste the notion of his own intellectual rigidity, of his perfect inability to receive new ideas and sensations, as one tastes an olive. The young dramatist, in a beautifully curved phrase, began to argue that certain emotional and purely intellectual experiences did not come under the axiom, but the librarian would have none of such a reservation. Then the women joined in, and it was just as if they had all five learnt off by heart one of Landor's lighter imaginary conversations, and were performing it. Well convinced that they were all five absurdly wrong, fanciful and sentimental either in optimism or pessimism, I nevertheless stood silent and barbaric. Could I cut across that lacework of shapely elegant sentences and apposite gestures with the jagged edge of what in England passes for a remark? The librarian was serious in his eternal frost. The dramatist had the air of being genuinely concerned about the matter; he spoke with deference to the librarian, with chivalrous respect to the women, and to me with glances of appeal for help; possibly the reason was that he was himself approaching the dreadful limit of twenty-five. But the women's eyes were always contradicting the polite seriousness of their tones. Their eyes seemed to be always mysteriously talking about something else; to be always saying: "All this that you are discussing is trivial, but I am brooding for ever on what alone is important." This, while true of nearly all women, is disturbingly true of Parisians. The ageing librarian, by dint of freezing harder, won the altercation: it was as though he stabbed them one by one with a dagger of ice. And presently he was lecturing them. The women were now admiring him. There was something in his face worn by maladies, in his frail physical unpleasantness, and in his frigid and total disgust with life, that responded to their secret dream. Their gaze caressed him, and he felt it falling on him like snow. That he intensely enjoyed his existence was certain.

They began talking low among themselves, the women, and there was an outburst of laughter; pretty giggling laughter. The two who had been at the piano stood aside and whispered and laughed with a more intimate intimacy, struggling to suppress the laughter, and yet every now and then letting it escape from sheer naughtiness. They cried. It was the *fou rire*. Impossible to believe that a moment before they had been performing in one of Landor's imaginary conversations, and that they were passionately serious about art and life and so on. They might have been schoolgirls.

"*Farceuses, toutes les deux!*" said the host, coming up, delightfully indulgent, but shocked that women to whom he had just played *Ygdrasil*, should be able so soon to throw off the spell of it.

The pretty and sprightly woman, all in white, despairing, whisked impulsively out of the room, in order to recall to herself amid darkness and cloaks and hats that she was not a giddy child, but an experienced creature of thirty if she was a day. She came back demure, her eyes liquid, brooding.

❖   ❖   ❖

"By the way," said the young dramatist to the host, "your People's Concert scheme – doesn't it move?"

"By the way," said the host, suddenly excited, "shall we hold a meeting of the committee now?"

He had a project for giving performances of the finest music to the populace at a charge of five sous per head. It was the latest activity of the publicist in him. The committee appeared to consist of everybody who was standing near. He drew me into it, because, coming from London, I was of course assumed to be a complete encyclopaedia of London and to be capable of furnishing detailed statistics about all twopence-halfpenny enterprises in London for placing the finest music before the people. The women, especially the late laughers, were touched by the beauty of the idea underlying the enterprise, and their eyes showed that at instants they were thinking sympathetically of the far-off "people". The librarian remained somewhat apart, as it were with a rifle, and maintained a desolating fire of questions: "Was the scheme meant to improve the people or to divert them? Would they come? Would they like the finest music? Why five sous? Why not seven, or three? Was the enterprise to be self-supporting?" The host, with his glance fixed in appeal on me (it seemed to me that he was entreating me to accept him as a serious publicist, warning me not to be misled by appearances) – the host replied to all these questions with the sweetest, politest, wistful patience, as well as he could. Certainly the people would like the finest music! The people had a taste naturally distinguished and correct. It was *we* who were the degenerates. The enterprise must be and would be self-supporting. No charity! No, he had learnt the folly of charity! But naturally the artists would give their services. They would be paid in terms of pleasure. The financial difficulty was that, whereas he would not charge more than five sous a head for admission, he could not hire a hall at a rent which worked out to less than a franc a head. Such was the problem before the committee meeting! Dufayel, the great shop-keeper, had offered to assist him. . . . The librarian frigidly exposed the anti-social nature of Dufayel's business methods, and the host hurriedly made him a present of Dufayel. Dufayel's help could not be conscientiously accepted. The problem then remained! . . . London? London, so practical? As an encyclopaedia of London I was not a success. Politeness hid a general astonishment that, freshly arrived from London, I could not suggest a solution, could not say what London would do in a like quandary, nor even what London had done!

"We will adjourn it to our next meeting," said the host, and named day, hour, and place. And the committee smoothed business out of its brow and dissolved itself, while at the host's request a girl performed some Japanese music on the Pleyel. When it was finished, the librarian, who had listened to Japanese music at an embassy, said that this was not Japanese music. "And thou knowest it well," he added. The host admitted that it was not really Japanese music, but he insisted with his plaintive smile that the whole subject of Japanese music was very interesting and enigmatic.

Then the pretty sprightly woman, all in white, went and stood behind an arm-chair and recited a poem, admirably, and with every sign of emotion. Difficult to believe that she had ever laughed, that she did not exist continually at these heights! She bowed modestly, a priestess of the poet, and came out from behind the chair.

"By whom?" demanded the librarian.

And a voice answered, throbbing: "Henri de Régnier."

"Indeed," said the librarian with cold, careless approval, "it is pretty enough."

But I knew, from the tone alone of the answering voice, that the name of Henri de Régnier was a sacred name, and that when it had been uttered the proper thing was to bow the head mutely, as before a Botticelli

"I have something here," said the host, producing one of those portfolios which hurried men of affairs carry under their arms in the streets of Paris, and which are called *serviettes*; this one, however, was of red morocco. The pretty, sprightly woman sprang forward blushing to obstruct his purpose, but other hands led her gently away. The host, using the back of the arm-chair for a lectern, read alternately poems of hers and poems of his own. And he, too, spoke with every sign of emotion. I had to conquer my instinctive British scorn for these people because they would not at any rate pretend that they were ashamed of the emotion of poetry. Their candour appeared to me, then, weak, if not actually indecent. The librarian admitted occasionally that something was pretty enough. The rest of the company maintained a steady fervency of enthusiasm. The reader himself forgot all else in his increasing ardour, and thus we heard about a score of poems – all, as we were told, unpublished – together with the discussion of a score of poems.

♦   ♦   ♦

We all sat around the rim of an immense circle of white tablecloth. Each on a little plate had a portion of pineapple ice and in a little glass a draught of Asti. Far away, in the centre of the diaper desert, withdrawn and beyond reach, lay a dish containing the remains of the ice. Except fans and cigarette-cases, there was nothing else on the table whatever. Some one across the table asked me what I had recently finished, and I said a play. Everybody agreed that it must be translated into French. The Paris theatres simply could not get good plays. In a few moments it was as if the entire company was beseeching me to allow my comedy to be translated and produced with dazzling success at one of the principal theatres on the boulevard. But I would not. I said my play was unsuitable for the French stage.

"Because?"

"Because it is too pure."

I had meant to be mildly jocular. But this joke excited mirth that surpassed mildness. "Thou hearest that? He says his play is too pure for us!" My belief is that they had never heard one of these strange, naive, puzzling barbarians make a joke before, and that they regarded the thing in its novelty as really too immensely and exotically funny, in some manner which they could not explain to themselves. Beneath their politeness I could detect them watching me, after that, in expectation of another outbreak of insular humour. I might have been tempted to commit follies, had not a new guest arrived. This was a tall, large-boned, ugly, coquettish woman, with a strong physical attractiveness and a voice that caused vibrations in your soul. She was in white, with a powerful leather waistband which suited her. She was intimate with everybody except me, and by a natural gift and force she held the attention of everybody from the moment of her entrance. You could see she was used to that. The time was a quarter to midnight, and she explained that she had been trying to arrive for hours, but could not have succeeded a second sooner. She said she must recount her *journée*, and she recounted her *journée*, which, after being a vague pre-historic nebulosity up to midday seemed to begin to take a definite shape about that hour. It was the *journée* of a Parisienne who is also an amateur actress and a dog-fancier. And undoubtedly all her days were the same: battles waged against clocks and destiny. She had no sense of order or of time. She had no exact knowledge of anything; she had no purpose in life; she was perfectly futile and useless. But she was acquainted with the secret nature of men and women; she could judge them shrewdly; she was the very opposite of the *ingénue*; and by her physical attractiveness, and that deep, thrilling voice, and her distinction of gesture and tone, she created in you the illusion that she was a capable and efficient woman, absorbed in the most important ends. She sat down negligently behind the host, waving away all ice and Asti, and busily fanning both him and herself. She flattered him by laying her ringed and fluffy arm along the back of his chair.

"Do you know," she said, smiling at him mysteriously, "I have made a strange discovery to-day. Paris gives more towards the saving of lost dogs than towards the saving of lost women. Very curious, is it not?"

The host seemed to be thunderstruck by this piece of information. The whole table was agitated by it, and a tremendous discussion was set on foot. I then witnessed for the first time the spectacle of a fairly large mixed company talking freely about scabrous facts. Then for the first time was I eased from the strain of pretending in a mixed company that things are not what they in fact are. To listen to those women, and to watch them listening, was as staggering as it would have been to see them pick up red-hot irons in their feverish, delicate hands. Their admission that they knew everything, that no corner of existence was dark enough to frighten them into speechlessness, was the chief of their charms, then. It intensified their acute femininity. And while they were thus gravely talking, ironical, sympathetic, amused, or indignant, they even yet had the air of secretly thinking about something else.

Discussions of such subjects never formally end, for the talkers never tire of them. This subject was discussed in knots all the way down six flights of stairs by the light of tapers and matches. I left the last, because I wanted to get some general information from my host about one of his guests.

"She is divorcing her husband," he said, with the simple sad pride of a man who has been a petitioner in the matrimonial courts. "For the rest, you never meet any but divorced women at my place. It saves complications. So have no fear."

We shook hands warmly.

"*Au revoir, mon ami.*"

"*Au revoir, mon cher.*"

A Tale of Tyranny

The Duval restaurants in Paris provided Bennett with notable experience. In the *Journal* on 5 October 1903 he wrote, "You can divide the restaurants of Paris, roughly, into two classes, those where the customers eat to live, and those where the customers eat to enjoy themselves. The Duvals are the great type of the former. . . ." On 18 November he wrote, "Last night, when I went into the Duval for dinner, a middle-aged woman, inordinately stout and with pendant cheeks, had taken the seat opposite to my prescriptive seat. . . ." The rest of the latter entry reflected upon the young and slim girl that the middle-aged woman must once have been, and imagined a sister for her who became a whore. Thus *The Old Wives' Tale* was conceived. The tale recorded below came to its crisis a few days later. It was published in *T.P.'s Weekly* on 25 March 1904 as one of a series of articles entitled "A Novelist's Log-Book". Bennett had it reprinted for friends in the third and last of his privately printed Christmas books, in 1908.

≥⦆   ≥⦆   ≥⦆

I trust that no reader will consider the following narrative trivial or deficient in emotional interest. It may, perhaps, seem so at first sight – this history of how a common working novelist came to be driven out of a restaurant – but I do not think that it really is so. I think that it would be well if more of such apparently simple episodes were stated and analysed, in order that light might be thrown upon an extremely obscure class of human relationships, namely, those relationships which are familiar and constant without being in the slightest degree intimate. It is, of course, for this high and philosophic reason, and not at all because I regard myself as an injured man, a man with a vivid grievance, that I am induced to set down the facts.

It is a good restaurant; and when I say that a restaurant is good, I who renew my flickering life almost solely in restaurants, the praise is deserved. It is large, quiet, clean, well-ventilated, well-warmed, well-decorated; the linen is good, the glass thin, the silver bright, and the service rapid; the raw material of the dishes is sound, and the dishes are well-cooked and various. I have nearly always enjoyed, and I have never disliked, what I ate in that restaurant. In short, it met with my hearty approval. There are, unhappily, precious few to match it in London, a city which has more inefficient restaurants to the square mile than any other city east of New York and west of Vladivostok.

She, too, was good. At any rate, I believe she was. Her dark hair was always most carefully dressed, her gowns fitted and suited her admirably; her features were agreeable, and her gestures showed kindness and force of character. Whether she was wife or widow, or neither, I could never decide, and I never asked her, though she once asked me if I was married. Nor did I know her name. I am, however, prepared to assert that she was over fifty in years, and that her waist-measurement was over forty. The first time our paths crossed in life's wilderness I omitted to give her the usual token of gratitude; but on the next evening, while seated at the table of quite another lady, I stopped her as she swept along carrying two calves' heads, a mutton-chop, Brussels sprouts, and a bottle of Burgundy, and I handed her a coin. She looked surprised. "For last night," I explained. Her face broke into a charming smile of recognition, a smile which entirely won me. From that moment I was hers.

Henceforth I sat always in a particular place, in her keeping. She told me what was particularly good in the menu, and she acquired a fairly exact knowledge of such of my idiosyncrasies as relate to sustentation. From my habit of invariably reading when I eat alone, I am apt to be regarded as one of those mooney and rapt individuals who are capable of forgetting whether or not they had dined, and this good woman would urge me to take my soup while it was hot, and so on. (Highly unnecessary advice.) Soon I became one of her flock. Every woman in her position has a flock of a dozen or a score men who are "hers" – and let all the restaurant take due note of it! At this point, or near it, the long tragedy began. I could not state accurately how the tragedy began – its inception was too subtle an affair – but I fancy it must have begun on the day when, in return for my coins, she said, "Thanks, young man!" I seemed to detect in the bluff, familiar phrase a slight misconception on her part as to my importance in the scheme of things. A few days more and I was admitted to the privilege of a regular familiarity.

She grumbled at me when I spilt the salt, pleasantly, maternally, good-naturedly; but still she grumbled. I was away travelling for a month, and when I came back she did not say, "Quite a stranger!" or anything of that sort. Without any preliminaries she said, "*Is she prettier than I am?*" It was wit, you know. I thought, "I must stop this." And having occasion to order French beans, I ordered French beans in a manner rather curt. "Well," she said, "that's a nice tone to order French beans in!" She smiled, but that was what she said. I said nothing. One night Another had taken her place, and I found myself hoping that she had found a distant sphere of usefulness. But the next night she was there just as usual, and as maternal, managing, and familiar as usual. With that moral courage, that ability to look a fact in the face which distinguishes me, I said to myself, "Mister, you're afraid of that woman."

Then a middle-aged man fell into the practice of dining exactly opposite to me, and he would insist on talking. He was the sort of middle-aged man who has made his way in the world, and formed positive opinions on everything, and whose positive opinions on everything, although sadly wrong, contain just enough superficial rightness to prevent you from crushing them without a long and intricate argument. He informed me that he was sixty-seven, and I looked at him. "Yes," he said, "you may look at me, but I am sixty-seven." He appeared about fifty. He was probably a peasant who had grown rich. I knew he was rich from his wines. He was a curious man. He would order beef *à la mode* and eat it, and then order a beefsteak and eat that. I never saw him either begin or finish a meal. He shaved, but his beard was evidently of strong growth, and I could only conclude that he shaved immediately before retiring for the night. Moreover, I disliked his method of eating peas. It was astonishing how that old man and She hit it off together. They both got on my nerves. "You call yourself a reasoning creature," I said to myself, "and yet you object to this excellent man merely because he shaves at night, orders a beefsteak after beef *à la mode*, and doesn't eat peas like you eat peas! How absurd! And you object to this kind-hearted, capable, bluff woman because – because her age is fifty and her waist forty! How preposterous!"

In one of Mr George Moore's distinguished novels someone says that you may grow to dislike a person to such a degree that that person can't walk across the room without annoying you. I achieved that degree with Her. And she never guessed it. She never knew that I didn't dote on her in my bashful, diffident way. And on a night it befell that the spiritual agony became too acute, and I was aware that I had entered that restaurant for the last time. And I had.

"Why," it may be asked, "did you not change your table? You say the restaurant was large." The answer is that I dared not. I dared not. Once I went in meaning to choose a different table and a different She; but the project failed; I had not the pluck. That woman, whose name I knew not and who knew not mine, who was nothing to me, to whom I had no obligations, who would have been compelled to suffer my desertion in silence – that woman had established a spiritual empire over me which I could only shake off by ceasing to see her. (And yet I have the reputation of being strong-minded, even brutal, in the pursuance of any course of conduct which I deem expedient.) She drove me out of a restaurant which I was genuinely sorry, and somewhat inconvenienced, to leave. If this is not an interesting and important fact bearing on the psychology of the sexes, I should humbly like to know what is. And as I write I feel that there is not a man who will not understand and sympathise with me, and not a woman who will not flout me.

Crude Life

Like "A Tale of Tyranny", the following essay was part of "A Novelist's Log-Book". It appeared in *T.P.'s Weekly* on 11 December 1903, and was reprinted in the Christmas book of 1908.

꧁ ꧁ ꧁

I fear that Paris and things Parisian often creep into the record of this journal, and that they will continue to do so. To explain the phenomenon I may as well state frankly that I have two domestic hearths, two sets of friends, two sets of tradesmen, two libraries, two loves, two everything. Let me add quickly that one love is London, the other Paris – merely that. (In my previous existence as a writer of *Savoir-Faire Papers,* I might have devoted an article to showing that, if one knows how, one may enjoy the advantages of a flat in London and a flat in Paris at a cost not exceeding the average cost of a single flat; but that incarnation, so intensely practical, is over and done with.) I spend much of my time in Paris because I like Paris and because I can work there. And yet the more intimately I know Paris the more I am impressed by the superior advantages of London, and by the fundamental superiority of the English character to the French, fine as the French people are. And this is not Chauvinism either: my views of patriotism resemble those of Sam Johnson and Grant Allen. I don't know why I should like Paris well enough to induce me to pay constantly the preposterous fares of the S.E. and C.R., or to

68

endure the refreshment accommodation on Dover pier, or the horrible jolting repasts on the Nord Railway. But I do. In justification I can only quote a fragment from Johnson's very fragmentary Journal of his visit to Paris: "Went on the boulevards. Saw nothing in particular, but was glad to be there." I think this states the case with Johnsonian terseness.

The other evening – to be precise, the very evening of the afternoon on which I wrote my Tale of Tyranny – I went to a little theatre in Montmartre. There are half-a-dozen or more little theatres within a stone's throw of my domestic hearth, where one can see relatively good plays relatively badly acted from an orchestra stall which costs at the most two francs. Note: All these theatres would be condemned by the L.C.C. as insanitary death-traps, and the L.C.C. would be wholly right. Still one goes. And in fairness to these little theatres "du quartier," one must admit that they are better than the regular theatres, in that they have no seats from which the stage is invisible. In fact, the audience is practically on the stage. The theatre which I visited is entitled "The Theatre of the People," and it lies on the very confines of "Parisianism," just at the point where the Avenue de Clichy ceases to be anything but a gaunt suburban thoroughfare. It is something rather wonderful, is the Theatre of the People, one of those enterprises at once glorious and forlorn, whose aim is to bring Art and the People together. The stalls are a franc, and the circles are half a franc, and the quality of the plays produced is decidedly high. Being a sort of duke, I hanged expense and procured an excessively special kind of *fauteuil* at an expenditure of one shilling and sevenpence halfpenny. The programme set before me included a two-act masterpiece of Molière, a one-act comedy by that truly great humourist Georges Courteline, and Heyermans' famous three-act tragedy of fisher life, *The Good Hope*. It was the last-named piece that I went to see. I had missed it when the Stage Society did it last year, and in doing it spent (I am told) one of the most melancholy and weeping afternoons that even the Stage Society has ever spent. I was anxious to witness the gloomy spectacle which had desolated every dramatic critic in London.

I came away from the theatre thoroughly and superbly depressed. *The Good Hope* is probably unrivalled for sheer gloom in the whole range of modern drama. But it was not *The Good Hope* that depressed me. *The Good Hope* is a good, sound play (and I adore gloom in art), and the entire performance was astonishingly artistic and satisfactory. What depressed me was the forlornness of the enterprise. The theatre was not half full, it was not a third full; and when we clapped (as we did often) our applause resounded as the voices of house-hunters resound in an empty house. And all the people connected with the enterprise, the programme women who had to live on microscopic tips, the cloakroom women who had to live on microscopic tips, and the refreshment-room waiter who had to live on microscopic tips, and the gentlemen "in front" who had to support dress-suits and families on perhaps twenty francs a week, all seemed to be wondering how long this Art-and-People game would last, and where their next meal was coming from. And I thought of the crowd of actors and actresses, all capable and apparently enthusiastic. (There wasn't above ten pounds in the theatre, and rent, electric light, royalties, advertising, mounting, costumes, to be taken out of that!) The whole glittering panorama of the Parisian stage seemed to be turned inside out before my eyes. One knows that in London a few flourish, while the rest struggle on by a species of weekly miracles. In Paris, the home of the theatre and of the theatre-goer, the state of affairs is twenty times worse; indeed, it is more tragic than the most tragic tragedy that Heyermans is likely to write. Why? No one can reasonably explain. I felt that in prolonging the illusion of those young actors and actresses even to the extent of one and sevenpence halfpenny I had been guilty of a social crime. I felt profoundly sorry for the whole pathetic crew; I became sentimental – and it is not often that I get sentimental. One actress – a certain Claire Mars (why had she borrowed that great name?) – stuck obstinately in my mind. She was not beautiful, but she was a star (of the Theatre of the People), and she could act, and she was intensely, too intensely, alive, and she was very young. She had the peculiar "yearning" eyes which always mean martyrdom, either for their owner or for some man.

And the next night the Theatre of the People was closed. And I read in the paper: "Suicide of a young actress of the Théâtre du Peuple. Mdlle. Lion, aged 23, committed suicide yesterday in her rooms, No. 40, Rue des Martyrs, by shooting herself in the right temple with a revolver. Under the name of

Claire Mars she had won applause in *Thérèse Raquin* and *The Good Hope*." Of the reason for this self-extinction I have no knowledge. Nor does the reason much matter. It is the raw event that counts. Logically, rationally, there is nothing strange in the fact that the vast secret forces which urge the universe from one day into the next should have brought just me to assist at the final grimaces of Mdlle. Lion – we were separated, she and I, only by a few feet and a line of electric light. And yet . . . what are logic and reason?

Of course, the affair is useless to me as a novelist. Art criticises life and rejects much that is too crude, too obvious, too red, for its purposes. Only the very great artist and the despicably small one dare to accept everything that life offers to them. Life is frequently all that art ought not to be. And that partly explains my annoyance when my friends exclaim to me: "Oh! I met such a *queer* character today. I wish you'd seen him. He certainly ought to go into a book!" But, as a human being, I allowed myself, after reading of the death of Mdlle. Mars, to think those well-known banal and commonplace thoughts about life and death which, despite their banality and commonplaceness, remain among the most precious and valuable of our emotions. And, in addition, I wondered how many people would not, at some moment or other, commit suicide if suicide could be committed instantaneously, without enterprise, sustained resolution, trouble, or mess. And it occurred to me that it is not death that most persons fear, but the business of dying. A lugubrious fragment of the journal, you will say. Well, and if it is? I must just tell you that today the posters of the Theatre of the People are crossed with a slip: "Immense Success!"

Monte

From 14 January to 12 February 1904 Bennett was at
Menton near Monte Carlo with Eden Phillpotts.
There they wrote a play called *Christina,* one of several
plays on which they collaborated that were never
produced. Their friends the novelists C. N. and
A. M. Williamson were staying at Monte Carlo.
Journal entries of the time record some of the details
that went into the following article, which was pub-
lished in *T.P.'s Weekly* on 12 and 19 February 1904.
It was reprinted in *Paris Nights.*

ᔐᕉ   ᔐᕉ   ᔐᕉ

Monte Carlo – the initiated call it merely "Monte" – has often
been described, in fiction and out of it, but the frank confession
of a ruined gambler is a rare thing; partly because the ruined
gambler can't often write well enough to express himself accurately, partly because he isn't in the mood for literary composition,
and partly because he is sometimes dead. So, since I am not dead,
and since it is only by means of literary composition that I can
hope to restore my shattered fortunes, I will give you the frank
confession of a ruined gambler. Before I went to Monte Carlo I
had all the usual ideas of the average sensible man about gambling
in general, and about Monte Carlo in particular. "Where does all
the exterior brilliance of Monte Carlo come from?" I asked sagely.
And I said further: "The Casino administration does not dis-

guise the fact that it makes a profit of about 50,000 francs a day.
Where does that profit come from?" And I answered my own
question with wonderful wisdom: "Out of the pockets of the
foolish gamblers." I specially despised the gambler who gambles
"on a system"; I despised him as a creature of superstition. For
the "system" gambler will argue that if I toss a penny up six
times and it falls "tail" every time, there is a strong probability
that it will fall "head" the seventh time. "Now," I said, "can any
rational creature be so foolish as to suppose that the six previous
and done-with spins can possibly affect the seventh spin? What
connection is there between them?" And I replied: "No rational
creature can be so foolish. And there is no connection." In this
spirit, superior, omniscient, I went to Monte Carlo.

Of course, I went to study human nature and find material. The
sole advantage of being a novelist is that when you are discovered
in a place where, as a serious person, you would prefer not to be
discovered, you can always aver that you are studying human
nature and seeking material. I was much impressed by the fact
of my being in Monte Carlo. I said to myself: "I am actually in
Monte Carlo!" I was proud. And when I got into the gorgeous
gaming saloons, amid that throng at once glittering and shabby,
I said: "I am actually in the gaming saloons!" And the thought at
the back of my mind was: "Henceforth I shall be able to say that I
have been in the gaming saloons at Monte Carlo." After studying
human nature at large, I began to study it at a roulette table.
I had gambled before – notably with impassive Arab chiefs in that
singular oasis of the Sahara desert, Biskra – but only a little, and
always at *petits chevaux*. But I understood roulette, and I knew
several "systems". I found the human nature very interesting;
also the roulette. The sight of real gold, silver, and notes flung
about in heaps warmed my imagination. At this point I felt a
solitary five-franc piece in my pocket. And then the red turned up
three times running, and I remembered a simple "system" that
began after a sequence of three.

◇   ◇   ◇

I don't know how it was, but long before I had formally decided
to gamble I knew by instinct that I should stake that five-franc
piece. I fought against the idea, but I couldn't take my hand empty

out of my pocket. Then at last (the whole experience occupying perhaps ten seconds) I drew forth the five-franc piece and bashfully put it on black. I thought that all the fifty or sixty persons crowded round the table were staring at me and thinking to themselves: "There's a beginner!" However, black won, and the croupier pushed another five-franc piece alongside of mine, and I picked them both up very smartly, remembering all the tales I had ever heard of thieves leaning over you at Monte Carlo and snatching your ill-gotten gains. I then thought: "This is a bit of all right. Just for fun I'll continue the system." I did so. In an hour I had made fifty francs, without breaking into gold. Once a croupier made a slip and was raking in red stakes when red had won, and people hesitated (because croupiers never make mistakes, you know, and you have to be careful how you quarrel with the table at Monte Carlo), and I was the first to give vent to a protest, and the croupier looked at me and smiled and apologised, and the winners looked at me gratefully, and I began to think myself the deuce and all of a Monte Carlo *habitué*.

Having made fifty francs, I decided that I would prove my self-control by ceasing to play. So I did prove it, and went to have tea in the Casino café. In those moments fifty francs seemed to me to be a really enormous sum. I was as happy as though I had shot a reviewer without being found out. I gradually began to perceive, too, that though no rational creature could suppose that a spin could be affected by previous spins, nevertheless, it undoubtedly was so affected. I began to scorn a little the average sensible man who scorned the gambler. "There is more in roulette than is dreamt of in your philosophy, my conceited friend," I murmured. I was like a woman – I couldn't argue, but I knew infallibly. Then it suddenly occurred to me that if I had gambled with louis instead of five-franc pieces I should have made 200 francs – 200 francs in rather over an hour! Oh, luxury! Oh, being-in-the-swim! Oh, smartness! Oh, gilded and delicious sin!

◇   ◇   ◇

Five days afterwards I went to Monte Carlo again, to lunch with some brother authors. In the meantime, though I had been chained to my desk by unalterable engagements, I had thought constantly

upon the art and craft of gambling. One of these authors knew
Monte Carlo, and all that therein is, as I know Fleet Street. And
to my equal astonishment and pleasure he said, when I explained
my system to him: "Couldn't have a better!" And he proceeded
to remark positively that the man who had a decent system and the
nerve to stick to it through all crises, would infallibly win from
the tables – not a lot, but an average of several louis per sitting of
two hours. "Gambling," he said, "is a matter of character. You
have the right character," he added. You may guess whether I did
not glow with joyous pride. "The tables make their money from
the plunging fools," I said, privately, "and I am not a fool." A
man was pointed out to me who extracted a regular income from
the tables. "But why don't the authorities forbid him the rooms?"
I demanded. "Because he's such a good advertisement. Can't you
see?" I saw.

We went to the Casino late after lunch. I cut myself adrift from
the rest of the party and began instantly to play. In forty-five
minutes, with my "system", I had made forty-five francs. And
then the rest of the party reappeared and talked about tea, and
trains, and dinner. "Tea!" I murmured disgusted (yet I have a
profound passion for tea), "when I am netting a franc a minute!"
However, I yielded, and we went and had tea at the Restaurant
de Paris across the way. And over the white-and-silver of the
tea-table, in the falling twilight, with the incomparable mountain
landscape in front of us, and the most *chic* and decadent Parisianism
around us, we talked roulette. Then the Russian Grand Duke who
had won several thousand pounds in a few minutes a week or two
before, came veritably and ducally in, and sat at the next table.
There was no mistaking his likeness to the Tsar. It is most extraordinary how the propinquity of a Grand Duke, experienced for
the first time, affects even the phlegm of a British novelist. I
seemed to be moving in a perfect atmosphere of Grand Dukes!
And I, too, had won! The art of literature seemed a very little thing.

◇   ◇   ◇

After I had made fifty and forty-five francs at two sittings, I
developed suddenly, without visiting the tables again, into a
complete and thorough gambler. I picked up all the technical

terms like picking up marbles – the greater martingale, the lesser martingale, "en plein", "a cheval", "the horses of seventeen", "last square", and so on, and so on – and I had my own original theories about the alleged superiority of red-or-black to odd-or-even in the betting on the even chances. In short, for many hours I lived roulette. I ate roulette for dinner, drank it in my Vichy, and smoked it in my cigar. At first I pretended that I was only pretending to be interested in gambling as a means of earning a livelihood (call it honest or dishonest, as you please). Then the average sensible man in me began to have rather a bad time, really. I frankly acknowledged to myself that I was veritably keen on the thing. I said: "Of course, ordinary people believe that the tables must win, but we who are initiated know better. All you want in order to win is a prudent system and great force of character." And I decided that it would be idle, that it would be falsely modest, that it would be inane, to deny that I had exceptional force of character. And beautiful schemes formed themselves in my mind: how I would gain a certain sum, and then increase my "units" from five-franc pieces to louis, and so quadruple the winnings, and how I would get a friend to practise the same system, and so double them again, and how generally we would have a quietly merry time at the expense of the tables during the next month.

And I was so calm, cool, collected, impassive. There was no hurry. I would not go to Monte Carlo the next day, but perhaps the day after. However, the next day proved to be very wet, and I was alone and idle, my friends being otherwise engaged, and hence I was simply obliged to go to Monte Carlo. I didn't wish to go, but what could one do? Before starting, I reflected: "Well, there's just a *chance* – such things have been known", and I took a substantial part of my financial resources out of my pocket-book, and locked that reserve up in a drawer. After this, who will dare to say that I was not cool and sagacious? The journey to Monte Carlo seemed very long. Just as I was entering the ornate portals I met some friends who had seen me there the previous day. The thought flashed through my mind: "These people will think I have got caught in the meshes of the vice just like ordinary idiots, whereas, of course, my case is not ordinary at all." So I quickly explained to them that it was very wet (as if they couldn't see), and that my other friends had left me, and that I had come to Monte

Carlo merely to kill time. They appeared to regard this explanation as unnecessary.

◇   ◇   ◇

I had a fancy for the table where I had previously played and won. I went to it, and by extraordinary good fortune secured a chair – a difficult thing to get in the afternoons. Behold me seated next door to a croupier, side by side with regular frequenters, regular practisers of systems, and doubtless envied by the outer ring of players and spectators! I was annoyed to find that every other occupant of a chair had a little printed card in black and red on which he marked the winning numbers. I had neglected to provide myself with this contrivance, and I felt conspicuous; I felt that I was not correct. However, I changed some gold for silver with the croupier, and laid the noble pieces in little piles in front of me, and looked as knowing and as initiated as I could. And at the first opening offered by the play I began the operation of my system, backing red, after black had won three times. Black won the fourth time, and I had lost five francs. . . . Black won the sixth time and I had lost thirty-five francs. Black won the seventh time, and I had lost seventy-five francs. "Steady, cool customer!" I addressed myself. I put down four louis (and kindly remember that in these hard times four louis is four louis – three English pounds and four English shillings), and, incredible to relate, black won the eighth time, and I had lost a hundred and fifty-five francs. The time occupied was a mere nine minutes. It was at this point that the "nerve" and the "force of character" were required, for it was an essential part of my system to "cut the loss" at the eighth turn. I said: "Hadn't I better put down eight louis and win all back again, *just this once*? Red's absolutely certain to win next time." But my confounded force of character came in, and forced me to cut the loss, and stick strictly to the system. And at the ninth spin red did win. If I had only put down that eight louis I should have been all right. I was extremely annoyed, especially when I realised that, even with decent luck, it would take me the best part of three hours to regain that hundred and fifty-five francs.

◇   ◇   ◇

I was shaken. I was like a pugilist who had been knocked down in a prize fight, and hasn't quite made up his mind whether, on the whole, he won't be more comfortable, in the long run, where he is. I was like a soldier under a heavy fire, arguing with himself rapidly whether he prefers to be a Balaclava hero with death or the workhouse, or just a plain, ordinary, prudent Tommy. I was stuck amidships. Then an American person behind my chair, just a casual foolish plunger, of the class out of which the Casino makes its profits, put a thousand franc note on the odd numbers, and thirty-three turned up. "A thousand for a thousand," said the croupier mechanically and nonchalantly, and handed to the foolish plunger the equivalent of eighty pounds sterling. And about two minutes afterwards the same foolish plunger made a hundred and sixty pounds at another single stroke. It was odious; I tell you positively it was odious. I collected the shattered bits of my character out of my boots, and recommenced my system; made a bit; felt better; and then zero turned up twice – most unsettling, even when zero means only that your stake is "held over". Then two old and fussy ladies came and gambled very seriously over my head, and deranged my hair with the end of the rake in raking up their miserable winnings. . . . At five o'clock I had lost a hundred and ninety-five francs. I don't mind working hard, at great nervous tension, in a vitiated atmosphere, if I can reckon on netting a franc a minute; but I have a sort of objection to three laborious sittings such as I endured that week when the grand result is a dead loss of four pounds. I somehow failed to see the point. I departed in disgust, and ordered tea at the Café de Paris, not the Restaurant de Paris (I was in no mood for Grand Dukes). And while I imbibed the tea, a heated altercation went on inside me between the average sensible man and the man who knew that money could be made out of the tables and that gambling was a question of nerves, etc. It was a pretty show, that altercation. In about ten rounds the average sensible man had knocked his opponent right out of the ring. I breathed a long breath, and seemed to wake up out of a nightmare. Did I regret the episode? I regretted the ruin, not the episode. For had I not all the time been studying human nature and getting material? Besides that, as I grow older I grow too wise. Says Montaigne: "*Wisdome hath hir excesses, and no leise need of moderation, then follie.*" (The italics are Montaigne's.) . . . And there's a good deal in my system after all.

Finishing a Book

When Bennett was writing *A Man from the North* in 1895 he described novel-writing to his friend George Sturt as "the damnedest, nerve shattering experience as ever was". Finishing a book cost him the greatest strain. He recorded in his journal how he wrote the last five thousand words of *Anna of the Five Towns* in seventeen hours of continuous work in May 1901, and how the writing of the last chapters of *Leonora* in June 1903 made him feel "as if the top of my head would come off". The book alluded to in the following article is presumably the comic novel *A Great Man*, which he finished writing on 13 March 1904. The article appeared in *T.P.'s Weekly* on 1 April 1904, and was reprinted in the Christmas book of 1908.

꿀 꿀 꿀

A little light will now be thrown on the real feelings of novelists, novelists who are not in the act and process of being interviewed, nor writing private diaries with one eye on posterity. A fortnight since I got into a peculiar state about my work, a sort of a fever. You may remember how England thrilled, a couple of years ago, over the marvellous tales of American bricklaying at the Westinghouse works at Manchester. I do not recall how many bricks each bricklayer laid per day, whether it was a thousand or a million; but I am sure that everyone had visions of bricklayers laying, laying, laying for dear life. I myself dreamt nightly of bricklayers laying at the final limit of speed, and snatching a hasty pint or so in between bricks. You will remember, too, the descriptions which are printed from time to time of feats of coaling in His Majesty's fleet; of vast, gigantic, and maddened coaling in which the entire personnel joins, from the Admiral to the Admiral's wife's maid; of coaling at the end of which all the coalers fall simultaneously down and go fast asleep on deck. And you will remember the speed of a horse when, towards evening, he turns into the road leading direct to his stable. If you amalgamate these impressions, and intensify them fivefold, you will have a notion of my state a fortnight back. Something drove me to work morning, noon, and night. There was no reason for it; indeed, it was indiscreet, because nothing is better calculated to give a fatal shock to a publisher than an author's delivery of a manuscript ahead of contract time, and no author likes a favourite publisher to die. My state can only be explained by Mr James Douglas's recent dictum in a weekly paper that English fiction has ceased to be an art, and is now a disease. I have it badly, and these particular symptoms of the dreadful malady recur about twice a year. I create new records daily of productiveness. The pace grows hotter and hotter. An accident seems inevitable, and then suddenly I stop. I come to my senses as a man emerges from a nightmare by falling out of bed. I experience a mild surprise. Oh, it is nothing! I have merely finished another book.

It is on the feelings which animate the novelist when he has finished a novel that I propose to make a few remarks. I can only speak positively for my own, but I have often questioned my brethren in disease, both great and small, and I find that mine represent about the average. My first feeling is certainly one of incredulity. "It can't really be true that I have finished the confounded thing." For you must observe that a novel wants a lot of writing. Fancy writing out in longhand all that print! How would you like to do it? As a matter of fact, the writing *is* a bore, and has a way of seeming interminable. So at first I am incredulous. My next feeling is a sudden feeling that takes me sharply like a pain in the back. The thought strikes me: "There's something peculiar in me today. What is it?" And then I remember: "Oh, yes, that book is finished." This feeling returns at intervals for several days.

So far I hope I have disturbed no one's cherished ideas; but what remains to say may cause annoyance to many who look at novels solely from the consumer's point of view. The dominant feeling in my mind is beyond question a feeling that I never want to see that book again, or any part of it, or to hear anything about it (except warm praise). And in particular I dismiss all the characters with profound relief. "For heaven's sake," I say to them, "depart utterly! I am sick of you! Do you hear? I am sick of you!" Yes, I say that even to the heroine, whose nobility of soul and true womanliness in the great renunciation chapter ought to move all hearts. I treat that unparalleled creature as though she were a scullion's wench. I have the right; no one else has. My attitude towards the unfortunate book is such that I fear the top of my head will come off if I am forced to correct the proofs, and I form wild schemes for asking some friend to do the proofs for me. Of course, this feeling becomes modified before the proofs actually arrive, and by the time the book is published I want so much to hear it talked about that I regard anyone who meets me and does not talk about it as guilty of a grave breach of manners. It may even occur to me to read the printed book for my own pleasure. I recall a passage that pleased me, and I say: "I'll just have a look at that." And I read and read on, and end by telling myself that the thing is simply wonderful. Its excellence surprises even me.

But regret at parting with the characters? No, no! When I read of Thackeray being plunged in grief at parting from the company in *Vanity Fair*, I murmured: "I know that grief. It is the sort of grief that the hostess expresses when she says she is so sorry you can't stay longer." I do not believe in the genuineness of that grief. (Agreed! I am fully aware that Thackeray was Thackeray, and that the last real novel was *Jude the Obscure*, and that I am only a charlatan, writing for so much a thousand, and diseased at that. Still, I exist; we exist, my brethren and I.) I repeat that I do not believe in the genuineness of that grief. A passing sentimental suspiration, a feeling of having lost something, of having been operated on for something severe, I would admit. But that Thackeray was not immensely glad to be rid of Dobbin, Amelia, Becky, and Co., I decline to believe. An author must pose; he can't help it. All artists must. A candid friend once abruptly finished a discussion with me by the remark: "Look here. You

know perfectly well it's part of your game to act the clown a bit."
For myself, my experience is that immediately one lot of characters has been kicked out another lot begins to collect in their place.
I have neither time nor inclination for those lifelong griefs
which authors who know how to cut a figure persuade themselves
that they have. I like my characters. I like them all, especially the
naughtiest, but I never encourage bumptiousness among them.
Liberties are not permitted. They know they are not real, and
I know they are not real.

Not real! Then (you say) they ought to be. Well, as a person who
devoted a considerable number of years to the study of the question,
I must gently ask to be allowed to differ. Characters are not real to
their authors. By which I mean that they do not give the illusion of
being real. They never did, and they never will. When an author
honestly and veritably mistakes a character for a real person, the
best thing that author can do is to go and see a doctor. You remind me that it is recorded that Balzac's characters were more
real to him than his friends and tradesmen. I am one of the most
passionate admirers of Balzac that ever lived, but I am certainly
not prepared to swallow that story. That was Balzac's way of
speaking, way of thinking. It was a *façon de parler*. It was a pose – a
pose which, like many poses, ended by imposing on the *poseur*.
It was part of the gorgeous Balzacian game. One has only to
imagine a case in order to satisfy oneself. Balzac was continually
having difficulties with publishers. Imagine that one of his publishers called upon him in the middle of the night (he worked
through the night), while he was engaged with old Goriot, or old
Grandet, or Lucien de Rubempré. Is anyone ready to argue that
Goriot or Grandet or Lucien would have seemed more real than
the publisher, or half as real? Balzac was in love for many years
with Madame de Hanska, whom he seldom saw. Had she surprised him by a sudden visit to Paris, would he have been in any
danger of falling into the arms of his Duchesse de Maufrigneuse
by mistake? Not much!

Journeys into the Forest

On 19 March 1904 Bennett visited his friend Henry Davray and his wife at Les Sablons near Moret, and they along with a Parisian physician, Dr Vallée, a friend of Bennett's, made one or both of the journeys into the forest recorded in the following essays. The *Journal* of that time reports some of the details. Later in 1904 Bennett leased rooms at Les Sablons for occasional use, and he and his wife spent the first months of their married life there, in the summer of 1907. In April 1908 they moved into the Villa des Néfliers near Fontainebleau. Bennett's love of the forest is reflected in many *Journal* references to it. In the summer of 1906 he made his ill-fated proposal to Eleanor Green there. In 1907–8 he composed parts of *The Old Wives' Tale* on solitary walks there.

The first essay was published in *T.P.'s Weekly* on 15 April 1904, under the title "The Secret of the Forest", and it was reprinted in the Christmas book of 1908 and again in *Paris Nights*. The second essay is known only from its publication in *Paris Nights*.

ﻬ﮿   ﻬ﮿   ﻬ﮿

First Journey into the Forest

Just to show how strange, mysterious and romantic life is, I will relate to you in a faithful narrative a few of my experiences the other day – it was a common Saturday. Some people may say that my experiences were after all quite ordinary experiences. After *all*, they were not. I was staying in a little house, unfamiliar to me, and beyond a radius of a few hundred yards I knew nothing of my surroundings, for I had arrived by train, and slept in the train. I felt that if I wandered far from that little house I should step into the unknown and the surprising. Even *in* the house I had to speak a foreign tongue; the bells rang in French. During the morning I walked about alone, not daring to go beyond the influence of the little house; I might have been a fly wandering within the small circle of lamplight on a tablecloth; all about me lay vast undiscovered spaces. Then after lunch a curious machine came by itself up to the door of the little house. I daresay you have seen these machines. You sit over something mysterious, with something still more mysterious in front of you. A singular liquid is poured into a tank; one drop explodes at a spark, and the explosion pushes the machine infinitesimally forward, another drop explodes and pushes the machine infinitesimally forward, and so on, and so on, and quicker and quicker, till you can out-strip trains. Such is the explanation given to me. I have a difficulty in believing it, but it seems to find general acceptance. However, the machine came up to the door of the little house, and took us off, four of us, all by itself; and after twisting about several lanes for a couple of minutes it ran us into a forest. I had somehow known all the time that that little house was on the edge of a great forest.

❖   ❖   ❖

Without being informed, I knew that it was a great forest, because against the first trees there was a large board which said "General Instructions for reading the signposts in the forest", and then a lot of details. No forest that was not a great forest, a mazy forest, and a dangerous forest to get lost in, would have had a notice board like that. As a matter of fact the forest was fifty miles in circumference. We plunged into it, further and further, exploding our way at the rate of twenty or thirty miles an hour, along a superb road which had a beginning and no end. Sometimes we saw a solitary horseman caracoling by the roadside; sometimes we passed a team of horses slowly dragging a dead tree; sometimes we heard the sound of a woodman's saw in the distance. Once or twice we detected a cloud of dust on the horizon of the road, and it came nearer and nearer, and proved to be a machine like ours, speeding on some mysterious errand in the forest. And as we progressed we looked at each other, and noticed that we were getting whiter and whiter – not merely our faces, but even our clothes. And for an extraordinary time we saw nothing but the road running away from under our wheels, and on either side trees, trees, trees – the beech, the oak, the hornbeam, the birch, the pine – interminable and impenetrable millions of them, prodigious in size, and holding strange glooms in the net of their leafless branches. And at intervals we passed cross-roads, disclosing glimpses, come and gone in a second, of other immense avenues of the same trees. And then, quite startlingly, quite without notice, we were out of the forest; it was just as if we were in a train and had come out of a tunnel.

And we had fallen into the midst of a very little village, sleeping on the edge of the forest, and watched over by a very large cathedral. Most of the cathedral had ceased to exist, including one side of the dizzy tower, but enough was left to instil awe. A butcher came with great keys (why a butcher, if the world is so commonplace as people make out?), and we entered the cathedral; and though outside the sun was hot, the interior of the vast fane was ice-cold, chilling the bones. And the cathedral was full of realistic statues of the Virgin, such as could only have been allowed to survive in an ice-cold cathedral on the edge of a magic forest. And then we climbed a dark corkscrew staircase for about an hour, and came out (as startlingly as we had come out of the forest) on the brink of a precipice two hundred feet deep. There was no rail. One little step, and that night our ghosts would have begun to haunt the remoter glades of the forest. The butcher laughed, and leaned over; perhaps he could do this with impunity because he was dressed in blue; I don't know.

❖   ❖   ❖

Soon afterwards the curious untiring machine had swept us into the forest again. And now the forest became more and more sinister, and beautiful with a dreadful beauty. Great processions of mighty and tremendous rocks straggled over hillocks, and made chasms and promontories, and lairs for tigers – tigers that burn bright in the night. But the road was always smooth, and it seemed nonchalant towards all these wonders. And presently it took us safely out of the forest once again. And this time we were in a town, a town that by some mistake of chronology had got into the wrong century; the mistake was a very gross one indeed. For this town had a fort with dungeons and things, and a moat all round it, and the quaintest streets and bridges and roofs and river craft. And processions in charge of nuns were walking to and fro in the grass-grown streets. And not only were the houses and shops quaint in the highest degree, but the shopkeepers also were all quaint. A grey-headed tailor dressed in black stood at the door of his shop, and his figure offered such a quaint spectacle that one of my friends and myself exclaimed at the same instant: "How Balzacian!" And we began to talk about Balzac's great novel *Ursule Mirouët*. It was as if that novel had come into actuality, and we were in the middle of it. Everything was Balzacian; those who have read Balzac's provincial stories will realise what that means. Yet we were able to buy modern cakes at a confectioner's. And we ordered tea, and sat at a table on the pavement in front of an antique inn. And close by us the landlady sat on a chair, and sewed, and watched us. I ventured into the great Balzacian kitchen of the inn, all rafters and copper pans, and found a pretty girl boiling water for our tea in one pan and milk for our tea in another pan. I told her it was wrong to boil the milk, but I could see she did not believe me. We were on the edge of the forest.

❖   ❖   ❖

And then the machine had carried us back into the forest. And this time we could see that it meant business. For it had chosen a road mightier than the others, and a road more determined to penetrate the very heart of the forest. We travelled many miles with scarcely a curve, until there were more trees behind us than a thousand men could count in a thousand years. And then – you know what happened next. At least you ought to be able to guess. We came to a castle. In the centre of all forests there is an enchanted castle, and there was an enchanted castle in the centre of this forest. And as the forest was vast, so was the castle vast. And as the forest was beautiful, so was the castle beautiful. It was a sleeping castle; the night of history had overtaken it. We entered its portals by a magnificent double staircase, and there was one watchman there, like a lizard, under the great doorway. He showed us the wonders of the castle, conducting us through an endless series of noble and splendid interiors, furnished to the last detail of luxury, but silent, unpeopled, and forlorn. Only the clocks were alive. "There are sixty-eight clocks in the castle." (And ever since I have thought of those sixty-eight clocks ticking away there, with ten miles of trees on every side of them.) And the interiors grew still more imposing. And at length we arrived at an immense apartment whose gorgeous and yet restrained magnificence drew from us audible murmurs of admiration. Prominent among the furniture was a great bed, hung with green and gold, and a glittering cradle; at the head of the cradle was poised a gold angel bearing a crown. Said the sleepy watchman: "Bed-chamber of Napoleon, with cradle of the King of Rome." This was the secret of the forest.

Of course it was all dreadfully ordinary. The forest was the Forest of Fontainebleau, and the castle was the palace thereof. And the cathedral was the well-known ruin of Larchant, and the town was the town of Nemours, where Balzac laid the scene of *Ursule Mirouët*. . . . Nevertheless, as I lay in bed that night in the little house on the edge of the forest, I thought thoughts which amounted to this: "What a planet we are on!"

Second Journey into the Forest

We glided swiftly into the forest as into a tunnel. But after a while could be seen a silvered lane of stars overhead, a ceiling to the invisible double wall of trees. There were these stars, the rush of tonic wind in our faces, and the glare of the low-hung lanterns on the road that raced to meet us. The car swerved twice in its flight, the second time violently. We understood that there had been danger. As the engine stopped, a great cross loomed up above us, intercepting certain rays; it stood in the middle of the road, which, dividing, enveloped its base, as the current of a river strokes an island. The doctor leaned over from the driving-seat and peered behind. In avoiding the cross he had mistaken for part of the macadam an expanse of dust which rain and wind had caked; and on this treachery the wheels had skidded. *"Ça aurait pu être une sale histoire!"* he said briefly and drily. In the pause we pictured ourselves flung against the cross, dead or dying. I noticed that other roads joined ours at the cross, and that a large grassy space, circular, separated us from the trees. As soon as we had recovered a little from the disconcerting glimpse of the next world, the doctor got down and re-started the engine, and our road began to race forward to us again, under the narrow ceiling of stars. After monotonous miles, during which I pondered upon eternity, nature, the meaning of life, the precariousness of my earthly situation, and the incipient hole in my boot-sole – all the common night-thoughts – we passed by a high obelisk (the primitive phallic symbol succeeding to the other), and turning to the right, followed an obscure gas-lit street of walls relieved by sculptured porticoes. Then came the vast and sombre courtyard of a vague palace, screened from us by a grille; we overtook a tramcar, a long, glazed box of electric light; and then we were suddenly in a bright and living town. We descended upon the terrace of a calm café, in front of which were ranged twin red-blossomed trees in green tubs, and a waiter in a large white apron and a tiny black jacket.

◈   ◈   ◈

The lights of the town lit the earth to an elevation of about fifteen feet; above that was the primeval and mysterious darkness, hiding even the house-tops. Within the planes of radiance people moved to and fro, appearing and disappearing on their secret errands; and glittering tramcars continually threaded the Square, attended by blue sparks. A monumental bull occupied a pedestal in the centre of the Square; parts of its body were lustrous, others intensely black, according to the incidence of the lights. My friends said it was the bull of Rosa Bonheur, the Amazon. Pointing to a dark void beyond the flanks of the bull, they said, too, that the palace was there, and spoke of the Council-Chamber of Napoleon, the cradle of the King of Rome, the boudoir of Marie Antoinette. I had to summon my faith in order to realise that I was in Fontainebleau, which hitherto had been to me chiefly a romantic name. In the deep and half-fearful pleasure of realisation – "This also has happened to me!" – I was aware of the thrill which has shaken me on many similar occasions, each however unique: as when I first stepped on a foreign shore; when I first saw the Alps, the Pyrenees; when I first strolled on the grand boulevards; when I first staked a coin at Monte Carlo; when I walked over the French frontier and read on a thing like a mile-post the sacred name "Italia"; and, most marvellous, when I stood alone in the Sahara and saw the vermilions and ochres of the Aurès Mountains. This thrill, ever returning, is the reward of a perfect ingenuousness.

◇   ◇   ◇

I was shown a map, and as I studied it, the strangeness of the town's situation seduced me more than the thought of its history. For the town, with its lights, cars, cafés, shops, halls, palaces, theatres, hotels, and sponging-houses, was lost in the midst of the great forest. Impossible to enter it, or to leave it, without winding through those dark woods! On the map I could trace all the roads, a dozen like ours, converging on the town. I had a vision of them, palely stretching through the interminable and sinister labyrinth of unquiet trees, and gradually reaching the humanity of the town. And I had a vision of the recesses of the forest, where the deer wandered or couched. All around, on the rim of the forest, were significant names: the Moret and the Grez and the Franchard of Stevenson; Barbizon; the Nemours of Balzac; Larchant. Nor did I forget the forest scene of George Moore's *Mildred Lawson*.

After we had sat half an hour in front of glasses, we rushed back through the forest to the house on its confines whence we had come. The fascination of the town did not cease to draw me until, years later, I yielded and went definitely to live in it.

Evening with Exiles

The evening described in the following sketch was in fact the evening of 28 September 1903, also a luncheon on 26 April 1904, also an evening on 6 May 1904, also a luncheon on 24 May 1904, and very probably other occasions. The *Journal* of the four dates records some of the details that Bennett drew upon, disguised, and perhaps embellished. The painter well known in Europe and America was probably taken mainly from the Canadian painter J. W. Morrice (1865–1924), who had lived in Paris since 1890, the Scotsman from the Irish painter Roderick O'Conor (1860–1940), who settled in France in 1883, Tommy Strutt from the English portrait painter Sir John Lavery (1856–1941), and the Mahatma from the eccentric poet Aleister Crowley (1875–1947). Very likely there is something of Sir Gerald Kelly (1879–1972) in one or another of the characterisations. Kelly went to Paris to study in 1901, and he and Bennett were acquainted. Crowley was married to Kelly's sister.

The sketch was published in the *English Review* in December 1910, and again in *Paris Nights*.

ᪧ   ᪧ   ᪧ

I lived up at the top of the house, absolutely alone. After eleven o'clock in the morning, when my servant left, I was my own doorkeeper. Like most solitaries in strange places, whenever I heard a ring I had a feeling that perhaps after all it might be the ring of romance. This time it was the telegraph-boy. I gave him a penny, because in France, much more than in England, everyone must live, and the notion still survives that a telegram has sufficient unusualness to demand a tip; the same with a registered letter. I read the telegram, and my evening lay suddenly in fragments at my feet. The customary accident, the accident dreaded by every solitary, had happened. "Sorry, prevented from coming to-night", etc. It was not yet six o'clock. I had in front of me a wilderness of six hours to traverse. In my warm disgust I went at once out in the streets. My flat had become mysteriously uninhabitable, and my work repugnant. The streets of Paris, by reason of their hospitality, are a refuge.

The last sun of September was setting across the circular Place Blanche. I sat down at the terrace of the smallest café and drank tea. Exactly opposite were the crimson wings of the Moulin Rouge, and to the right was the establishment which then held first place among nocturnal restaurants in Montmartre. It had the strange charm of a resort which is never closed, night or day, and where money and time are squandered with infantile fatuity. Somehow it inspired respect, if not awe. Its terrace was seldom empty, and at that hour it was always full. Under the striped and valanced awning sat perhaps a hundred people, all slowly and deliberately administering to themselves poisons of various beautiful colours. A crowd to give pause to the divination of even the most conceited student of human nature, a crowd in which the simplest bourgeois or artist or thief sat next to men and women exercising the oldest and most disreputable professions – and it was impossible surely to distinguish which from which!

Out of the medley of trams, omnibuses, carts, automobiles, and cabs that continually rattled over the cobbles, an open *fiacre* would detach itself every minute or so, and set down or take up in front of the terrace. Among these was one carrying two young dandies, an elegantly dressed girl, and another young girl in a servant's cap and apron. They were all laughing and talking together. The dandies and the elegancy got out and took a vacant table amid the welcoming eager bows of a *maître d'hôtel*, a *chasseur*, and a waiter. She was freshly and meticulously and triumphantly got up, like an elaborate confection of starched linen fresh from the laundress. Her lips were impeccably rouged. She delighted the eye by her health and her youth and her pretty insolence. A single touch would have soiled her, but she had not yet been touched. Her day had just begun. Probably, her bed was not yet made. The black-robed, scissored girls of the drapery store at the next angle of the *place* were finishing their tenth hour of vigil over goods displayed on the footpath. And next to that was a creamery where black-robed girls could obtain a whole day's sustenance for the price of one glass of poison. Evidently the young creature had only just arrived at the dignity of a fashionable dressmaker, and a servant of her own. Her ingenuous vanity obliged her to show her servant to the *place*, and the ingenuous vanity of the servant was content to be shown off; for the servant might have a servant to-morrow – who could tell? The cabman and the servant began to converse, and presently the cabman in his long fawn coat and white hat descended and entered the vehicle and sat down by the servant, and pulled out an illustrated comic paper, and they bent their heads over it and giggled enormously in unison; he was piling up money at the rate of at least a sou a minute. Occasionally the young mistress threw a loud sisterly remark to the servant, who replied gaily. And the two young dandies bore nobly the difficult *rôle* of world-worn men who still count not the cost of smiles. Say what you like, it was charming. It was one of the reasons why Paris is the city which is always forgiven. Could one reasonably expect that the bright face of the vapid little siren should be solemnised by the thought: "To-day I am a day nearer forty than I was yesterday"?

The wings of the Moulin Rouge, jewelled now with crimson lamps, began to revolve slowly. The upper chambers of the restaurant showed lights behind their mysteriously-curtained windows. The terrace was suddenly bathed in the calm blue of electricity. No austere realism of the philosopher could argue away the romance of the scene.

❖   ❖   ❖

I turned down the steep Rue Blanche, and at the foot of it passed by the shadow of the Trinité, the great church of illicit assignations, at whose clock scores of frightened and expectant hearts gaze anxiously every afternoon; and through the Rue de la Chaussée d'Antin, where corsets are masterpieces beyond price and flowers may be sold for a sovereign apiece, and then into the full fever of the grand boulevard with its maddening restlessness of illuminated signs. The shops and *cafés* were all on fire, making two embankments of fire, above which rose high and mysterious façades masked by trees that looked like the impossible verdure of an opera. And between the summits of the trees a ribbon of rich, dark, soothing purple – the sky! This was the city. This was what the race had accomplished after eighteen Louis and nearly as many revolutions, and when all was said that could be said it remained a prodigious and a comforting spectacle. Every doorway shone with invitation; every satisfaction and delight was offered, on terms ridiculously reasonable. And binding everything together were the refined, neighbourly, and graceful cynical gestures of the race: so different from the harsh and awkward timidity, the self-centred egotism and aristocratic hypocrisy of Piccadilly. It seemed difficult to be lonely amid multitudes that so candidly accepted human nature as human nature is. It seemed a splendid and an uplifting thing to be there. I continued southwards, down the narrow swarming Rue Richelieu, past the immeasurable National Library on the left and Jean Goujon's sculptures of the rivers of France on the right, and past the Théâtre Français, where nice plain people were waiting to see *L'Aventurière,* and across the arcaded Rue de Rivoli. And then I was in the dark desert of the Place du Carrousel, where the omnibuses are diminished to toy-omnibuses. The town was shut off by the vast arms of the Louvre. The purple had faded from out the sky. The wind, heralding October, blew coldly across the spaces. The artfully arranged vista of the Champs Elysées, rising in flame against the silhouette of Cleopatra's needle, struck me as a meretricious device, designed to impress tourists and monarchs. Everything was meretricious. I could not even strike a match without being reminded that a contented and corrupt inefficiency was corroding this race like a disease. I could not light my cigarette because somebody, somewhere, had not done his job like an honest man. And thus it was throughout.

I wanted to dine, and there were a thousand restaurants within a mile; but they had all ceased to invite me. I was beaten down by the overwhelming sadness of one who for the time being has no definite arranged claim to any friendly attention in a huge city – crowded with pre-occupied human beings. I might have been George Gissing. I re-wrote all his novels for him in an instant. I persisted southwards. The tiny walled river, reflecting with industrious precision all its lights, had no attraction. The quays, where all the book shops were closed and all the bookstalls locked down, and where there was never a *café*, were as inhospitable and chill as Riga. Mist seemed to heave over the river, and the pavements were oozing damp.

I went up an entry and rang a bell, thinking to myself: "If he isn't in, I am done for!" But at the same moment I caught the sound of a violoncello, and I knew I was saved, and by a miracle Paris was herself again.

✧   ✧   ✧

"Not engaged for dinner, are you?" I asked, as soon as I was in the studio.

"No. I was just thinking of going out."

"Well, let's go, then."

"I was scraping some bits of Gluck."

The studio was fairly large, but it was bare, unkempt, dirty and comfortless. Except an old sofa, two hard imperfect chairs, and an untrustworthy table, it had no furniture. Of course, it was littered with the apparatus of painting. Its sole ornamentation was pictures, and the pictures were very fine, for they were the painter's own. He and his pictures are well known among the painters of Europe and America. Successful artistically, and with an adequate private income, he was a full member of the Champ de Mars Salon, and he sold his pictures upon occasion to Governments. Although a British subject, he had spent nearly all his life in Paris; he knew the streets and resorts of Paris like a Frenchman; he spoke French like a Frenchman. I never heard of him going to England. I never heard him express a desire to go to England. His age was perhaps fifty, and I dare say that he had lived in that studio for a quarter of a century, with his violoncello. It was plain, as he stood there well dressed, and with a vivacious and yet dreamy eye, that the zest of life had not waned in him. He was a man who, now as much as ever, took his pleasure in seeing and painting beautiful, suave, harmonious things. And yet he stood there unapologetic amid that ugly and narrow discomfort, with the sheet of music pinned carelessly to an easel, and lighted by a small ill-regulated lamp with a truncated, dirty chimney – sole illumination of the chamber! His vivacious and dreamy eye simply did not see all that, never had seen it, never saw anything that it did not care to see. Nobody ever heard him multiply words about a bad picture, for example, – he would ignore it.

With a gesture of habit that must have taken years to acquire he took a common rose-coloured packet of caporal cigarettes from the table by the lamp and offered it to me, pushing one of the cigarettes out beyond its fellows from behind; you knew that he was always handling cigarettes.

"It's not really arranged for 'cello," he murmured, gazing at the music, which was an air from *Alceste*, arranged for violin. "You see it's in the treble clef."

"I wish you'd play it," I said.

He sat down and played it, because he was interested in it. With his greying hair and his fashionable grey suit, and his oldest friend, the brown 'cello, gleaming between his knees, he was the centre of a small region of light in the gloomy studio, and the sound of the 'cello filled the studio. He had no home; but if he had had a home this would have been his home, and this his home-life. As a private individual, as distinguished from a public artist, this was what he had arrived at. He had secured this refuge, and invented this relaxation, in the middle of Paris. By their aid he could defy Paris. There was something wistful about the scene, but it was also impressive, at any rate to me, who am otherwise constituted. He was an exile in the city of exiles; a characteristic item in it, though of a variety exceedingly rare. But he would have been equally an exile in any other city. He had no consciousness of being an exile, of being homeless. He was above patriotisms and homes. Why, when he wanted even a book he only borrowed it!

"Well, shall we go out and eat?" I suggested, after listening to several lovely airs.

"Yes," he said, "I was just going. I don't think you've seen my last etching. Care to?"

I did care to see it, but I also desired my dinner.

"This is a pretty good print, but I shall get better," he said, holding the sheet of paper under the lamp.

"How many shall you print?" I asked.

"Thirty."

"You might put me down for one."

"All right. I think it will give you pleasure," he said with impartial and dignified conviction.

After another ten minutes, we were out on the quay.

"Grand autumn night," he said appreciatively. "Where shall we have the *apéritif*?"

"*Apéritif!* It's after eight o'clock, man!"

" I think we shall have time for an *apéritif*," he insisted, mildly shocked.

Drawing-rooms have their ritual. His life, too, had its ritual.

❖   ❖   ❖

At nearly midnight we were sitting, three of us, in a *café* of the Montparnasse quarter, possibly the principal *café* of the Montparnasse quarter. Neither notorious nor secretly eccentric; but an honest *café*, in the sense of "honest" applied to certain women. Being situated close to a large railway terminus, it had a broad and an indulgent attitude towards life. It would have received a frivolous *habitué* of the Place Blanche, or a nun, or a clergyman, with the same placidity. And although the district was modified, and whole streets, indeed, de-Parisianised by wandering cohorts of American and English art-amateurs of both sexes, this *café* remained, while accepting them, characteristically French. The cohorts thought they were seeing French life when they entered it; and they in fact were.

This *café* was the chief club of the district, with a multitudinous and regular *clientèle* of billiard-players, card-players, draughts-players, newspaper readers, chatterers, and simple imbibers of bock. Its doors were continually a-swing, and one or the other of the two high-enthroned *caissières* was continually lifting her watchful head from the desk to observe who entered. Its interior seemed to penetrate indefinitely into the hinterland of the street, and the effect of unendingness was intensified by means of mirrors, which reflected the shirt-sleeved arms and the cues of a score of billiard-players. Everywhere the same lively and expressive and never ungraceful gestures, between the marble-tops below and the light-studded ceiling above! Everywhere the same murmur of confusing pleasant voices broken by the loud chant of waiters intoning orders at the service-bar, and by the setting down of heavy glass mugs and saucers upon marble! Over the *café*, unperceived, unthought of, were the six storeys of a large house comprising perhaps twenty-five separate and complete homes.

The third man at our table was another exile, also a painter, but a Scotchman. He had lived in Paris since everlasting, but before that rumour said that he had lived for several years immovable at the little inn of a Norman village. Now, he never left Paris, even in summer. He exhibited, with marked discretion, only at the Indépendants. Beyond these facts, and the obvious fact that he enjoyed independent means, nobody knew anything about him save his opinions. Even his age was exceedingly uncertain. He looked forty, but there were acquaintances who said that he had looked forty for twenty years. He was one of those extremely reserved men who talk freely. Of his hopes, ambitions, ideals, disappointments, connections, he never said a word, but he did not refuse his opinion upon any subject, and on every subject he had a definite opinion which he would express very clearly, with a sort of polite curtness. His tendency was to cynicism – too cynical to be bitter. He did not complain of human nature, but he thoroughly believed the worst of it. These two men, the 'cellist and the Scotchman, were fast friends; or rather – as it might be argued in the strict sense neither of them had a friend – they were very familiar acquaintances; each with a profound respect for the other's judgment admired his companion for a genius, as everybody did.

They talked together for ever and ever, but not about politics. They were impatient on politics. Both were apparently convinced that politics are an artificiality imposed upon society by adventurers and interferers, and that if such people could be exterminated politics would disappear. Certainly neither had any interest in the organic aspect of society. Their political desire was to be let alone. Nor did they often or for long "talk bawdy"; after opinions had been given which no sensible man ever confides to more than two reliable others at a time, the Scotchman would sweep all that away as secondary. Nor did they talk of the events of the day, unless it might be some titillating crime or mystery such as will fill whole pages of the newspaper for a week together. They talked of the arts, all the arts. And although they seemed to be always either in that *café*, or in their studios, or in bed, they had the air of being mysteriously but genuinely abreast of every manifestation of art. And since all the arts are one, and in respect to art they had a real attitude and real views, all that they said was valuable suggestively, and their ideas could not by any prodigality be exhausted. As a patron of the arts even the State interested them, and herein they showed glimmerings of a social sense. In the intervals of this eternal and absorbing "art", they would discuss with admirable restrained gusto the exacerbating ridiculousness of the cohorts of American and English art-amateurs who infested and infected the quarter.

❖   ❖   ❖

Little bands of these came into the *café* from time to time, and drifting along the aisles of chairs would sit down where they could see as much as possible with their candid eyes. The girls, inelegant and blousy; the men, inept in their narrow shrewdness: both equally naive, conceited, uncorrupted and incorruptible, they were absolutely incapable of appreciating the refined and corrupt decadence, the stylistic charm, the exquisite tradition of the civilisation at which they foolishly stared, as at a peepshow. Not a thousand years would teach them the human hourly art of life as it was subtly practised by the people whose very language they disdained to learn. When loud fragments of French phrases, massacred by Americans who had floated on but not mingled with Paris for years, reached us from an Anglo-Saxon table, my friends would seem to shudder secretly, ashamed of being Anglo-Saxon. And if they were obliged to salute some uncouth Anglo-Saxon acquaintance, and thus admit their own un-Latin origin, their eyes would say: "Why cannot these people be imprisoned at home? Why are not we alone of Anglo-Saxons permitted to inhabit Paris?"

Occasionally a bore would complacently present himself for sufferance. Among these the chief was certainly the man whose existence was an endless shuttle-work between the various cities where art is or has been practised, from Munich to Naples. He knew everything about painting, but he ought to have been a bookmaker. He was notorious everywhere as the friend of Strutt, Strutt being the very famous and wealthy English portrait-painter of girls. All his remarks were *à propos* of Tommy Strutt, Tommy Strutt – Tommy. He was invariably full of Tommy. And this evening he was full of Tommy's new German model, whose portrait had been in that year's Salon. . . . How Tommy had picked her up in the streets of Berlin; how she was nineteen, and the rage of Berlin, and was asked to lunch at the embassies, and had received five proposals in three months; how she refused to sit for any one but Tommy, and even for him would only sit two hours a day: how Tommy looked after her, and sent her to bed at nine-thirty of a night, and hired a woman to play with her; and how Tommy had once telegraphed to her that he was coming to Berlin, and how she had hired a studio and got it painted and furnished exactly to his fastidious taste all on her own, and met him at the station and driven him to the studio, and tea was all ready, etc.; and how pretty she was. . . .

"What's her figure like?" the Scotchman inquired gruffly.

"The fact is," said Tommy's friend, dashed, "I haven't seen her posing for the nude. I've seen her posing to Tommy in a bathing-costume on the seashore, but I haven't yet seen her posing for the nude. . . ." He became reflective. "My boy, do you know what my old uncle used to say to me down at the old place in Kildare, when I was a youngster? My old uncle used to say to me – and he was dying – 'My boy, I've always made a rule of making love to every pretty woman I met. It's a sound rule. But let me warn you – you mustn't expect to get more than five per cent on your outlay!' "

" 'The old place in Kildare!' " murmured the Scotchman, in a peculiarly significant tone, after Tommy Strutt's friend had gone; and this was the only comment on Tommy Strutt's friend.

❖   ❖   ❖

The talk on art was resumed, the renowned Tommy Strutt being reduced to his proper level of the third-rate and abruptly dismissed. One o'clock! A quarter past one! The *café* was now nearly empty. But these men had no regard for time. Time did not exist for them, any more than the structure of society. They were not bored, nor tired. They conversed with ease, and with mild pleasure in their own irony and in the disillusioned surety of their judgments. Then I noticed that the waiters had dwindled to two, and that only one cashier was left enthroned behind the bar; somewhat later, she too had actually gone! Both had at length rejoined their families, if any. The idea was startling that these prim and neat and mechanically smiling women were human, had private relations, a private life, a bed, a wardrobe. All over Paris, all day, every day, they sit and estimate the contents of trays, which waiters present to their practised gaze for an instant only, and receive the value of the drinks in bone discs, and write down columns of figures in long ledgers. They never take exercise, nor see the sun; they even eat in the *café*. Mystic careers! . . . A quarter to two. Now the chairs had been brought in from the terrace, and there was only one waiter, and no other customer that I could see. The waiter, his face nearly as pale as his apron, eyed us with patient and bland resignation, sure from his deep knowledge of human habits that sooner or later we should in fact depart, and well inured to the great Parisian principle that a *café* exists for the convenience of its *habitués*. I was uneasy: I was even aware of guiltiness; but not my friends.

Then a face looked in at the doorway, as if reconnoitring, and hesitated.

"By Jove!" said the violoncellist. "There's the Mahatma back again! Oh! He's seen us!"

The peering face preceded a sloping body into the *café*, and I was introduced to a man whose excellent poems I had read in a limited edition. He was wearing a heavily jewelled red waistcoat, and the largest ring I ever saw on a human hand. He sat down. The waiter took his order and intoned it in front of the service-bar, proving that another fellow-creature was hidden there awaiting our pleasure. When the Mahatma's glass was brought, the Scotchman suddenly demanded from the waiter the total of our modest consumption, and paid it. The Mahatma said that he had arrived that evening direct from the Himalayas, and that he had been made or ordained a "khan" in the East. Without any preface he began to talk supernaturally. As he had known Aubrey Beardsley,

I referred to the rumour that Beardsley had several times been seen abroad in London after his alleged death.

"That's nothing," he said quickly. "I know a man who saw and spoke to Oscar Wilde in the Pyrenees at the very time when Oscar was in prison in England."

"Who was the man?" I inquired.

He paused. "Myself," he said, in a low tone.

"Shall we go?" The Scotchman, faintly smiling, embraced his friend and me in the question.

We went, leaving the Mahatma bent in solitude over his glass. The waiter was obviously saying to himself: "It was inevitable that they should ultimately go, and they have gone." We had sat for four hours.

Outside, cabs were still rolling to and fro. After cheerful casual good-nights, we got indolently into three separate cabs, and went our easy ways. I saw in my imagination the vista of the thousands of similar nights which my friends had spent, and the vista of the thousands of similar nights which they would yet spend. And the sight was majestic, tremendous.

The Secret of Content

The following essay was the last of the "Savoir-Vivre Papers" (successor to the "Savoir-Faire Papers"), and appeared in *T.P.'s Weekly* on 28 September 1906. It was reprinted in *The Reasonable Life* in 1907, and again in *Mental Efficiency* (an enlarged form of *The Reasonable Life*) in 1912.

For me, spiritual content (I will not use the word "happiness", which implies too much) springs essentially from no mental or physical facts. It springs from the spiritual fact that there is something higher in man than the mind, and that that something can control the mind. Call that something the soul, or what you will. My sense of security amid the collisions of existence lies in the firm consciousness that just as my body is the servant of my mind, so is my mind the servant of *me*. An unruly servant, but a servant – and possibly getting less unruly every day! Often have I said to that restive brain: "Now, O mind, sole means of communication between the divine *me* and all external phenomena, you are not a free agent; you are a subordinate; you are nothing but a piece of machinery; and obey me you *shall*."

The mind can only be conquered by regular meditation, by deciding beforehand what direction its activity ought to take, and insisting that its activity takes that direction; also by never leaving it idle, undirected, masterless, to play at random like a child in the streets after dark. This is extremely difficult, but it can be done, and it is marvellously well worth doing. The fault of the epoch is the absence of meditativeness. A sagacious man will strive to correct in himself the faults of his epoch. In some deep ways the twelfth century had advantages over the twentieth. It practised meditation. The twentieth does Sandow exercises. Meditation (I speak only for myself) is the least dispensable of the day's doings. What do I force my mind to meditate upon? Upon various things, but chiefly upon one.

Namely, that Force, Energy, Life – the Incomprehensible has many names – is indestructible, and that, in the last analysis, there is only one single, unique Force, Energy, Life. Science is gradually reducing all elements to one element. Science is making it increasingly difficult to conceive matter apart from spirit. Everything lives. Even my razor gets "tired". And the fatigue of my razor is no more or less explicable than my fatigue after a passage of arms with my mind. The Force in it, and in me, has been transformed, not lost. All Force is the same force. Science just now has a tendency to call it electricity; but I am indifferent to such baptisms. The same Force pervades my razor, my cow in my field, and the central *me* which dominates my mind: the same force in different stages of evolution. And that Force persists for ever. In such paths do I compel my mind to walk daily. Daily it has to recognise that the mysterious Ego controlling it is a part of that divine Force which exists from everlasting to everlasting, and which, in its ultimate atoms, nothing can harm. By such a course of training, even the mind, the coarse, practical mind, at last perceives that worldly accidents don't count.

"But," you will exclaim, "this is nothing but the immortality of the soul over again!" Well, in a slightly more abstract form, it is. (I never said I had discovered anything new.) I do not permit myself to be dogmatic about the persistence of personality, or even of individuality after death. But, in basing my physical and mental life on the assumption that there is something in me which is indestructible and essentially changeless, I go no further than science points. Yes, if it gives you pleasure, let us call it the immortality of the soul. If I miss my train, or my tailor disgraces himself, or I lose that earthly manifestation of Force that happens to be dearest to me, I say to my mind: "Mind, concentrate your powers upon the full realisation of the fact that I, your master, am immortal and beyond the reach of accidents." And my mind, knowing by this time that I am a hard master, obediently does so. Am I, a portion of the Infinite Force that existed billions of years ago, and which will exist billions of years hence, going to allow myself to be worried by any terrestrial physical or mental event? I am not. As for the vicissitudes of my body, that servant of my servant, it had better keep its place, and not make too much fuss. Not that any fuss occurring in either of these outward envelopes of the eternal *me* could really disturb me. The eternal is calm; it has the best reason for being so.

So you say to yourselves: "Here is a man in a penny weekly paper advocating daily meditation upon the immortality of the soul as a cure for discontent and unhappiness! A strange phenomenon!" That it should be strange is an indictment of the epoch. My only reply to you is this: Try it. Of course, I freely grant that such meditation, while it "casts out fear", slowly kills desire and makes for a certain high indifference; and that the extinguishing of desire, with an accompanying indifference, be it high or low, is bad for youth. But I am not a youth, and to-day I am writing for those who have tasted disillusion: which youth has not. Yet I would not have you believe that I scorn the brief joys of this world. My attitude towards them would fain be that of Socrates, as stated by the incomparable Marcus Aurelius: "He knew how to lack, and how to enjoy, those things in the lack whereof most men show themselves weak; and in the fruition, intemperate."

Besides commanding my mind to dwell upon the indestructible and final omnipotence of the Force which is me, I command it to dwell upon the logical consequences of that *unity* of force which science is now beginning to teach. The same essential force that is *me* is also *you*. Says the Indian proverb: "I met a hundred men on the road to Delhi, and they were all my brothers." Yes, and they were all my twin brothers, if I may so express it, and a thousand times closer to me even than the common conception of twin brothers. We are all of us the same in essence; what separates us is merely differences in our respective stages of evolution. Constant reflection upon this fact must produce that universal sympathy which alone can produce a positive content. It must do away with such ridiculous feelings as blame, irritation, anger, resentment. It must establish in the mind an all-embracing tolerance. Until a man can look upon the drunkard in his drunkenness, and upon the wife-beater in his brutality, with pure and calm compassion; until his heart goes out instinctively to every other manifestation of the unique Force; until he is surcharged with an eager and unconquerable benevolence towards everything that lives; until he has utterly abandoned the presumptuous practice of judging and condemning – he will never attain real content. "Ah!" you exclaim again, "he has nothing newer to tell us than that 'the greatest of these is charity'!" I have not. It may strike you as excessively funny, but I have discovered nothing newer than that. I merely remind you of it. Thus it is, twins on the road to Delhi, by continual meditation upon the indestructibility of Force, that I try to cultivate calm, and by continual meditation upon the oneness of Force that I try to cultivate charity, being fully convinced that in calmness and in charity lies the secret of a placid if not ecstatic happiness. It is often said that no thinking person can be happy in this world. My view is that the more a man thinks the more happy he is likely to be. I have spoken. I am overwhelmingly aware that I have spoken crudely, abruptly, inadequately, confusedly.

The Rising Storm of Life

During his years in France, Bennett usually visited England once every six months or so. On Sunday, 14 June 1907, he returned to see his mother in Burslem, to tell her of his impending marriage. The following article appeared on 5 July 1907, the day after his marriage, in *T.P.'s Weekly*. Just three months later he began writing *The Old Wives' Tale*.

ᘓᕲ   ᘓᕲ   ᘓᕲ

Last Sunday I came fresh into England and London after a long absence. It was a windy, sunshiny day, and everything in London seemed to be moving as fast as the wind. There was a vigorous gaiety in the air: I could see it in the quivering flags that stood out straight over high edifices, and in the motor omnibuses as they swept past in long rattling curves like ships with all their bolts loose, and in the bright, adventurous costumes of the women. When I had climbed to the upper deck of one of these street-steamers, I sat at gaze, fighting for my hat with the wind, as the machine, grandly rolling, swirled me across Trafalgar Square, and I said to myself, "Is this London, and Sunday?"

For the streets were full of new blouses and new neckties and smiles. And all around immense buildings were rising behind poles; I could almost see them rising – buildings devoted to pleasure; their knees were swathed in white and coloured posters, calling the new London to pleasure. And I could almost see the lifts ascending and descending in a thousand hotels, and I could almost see the electric trains flitting about in their lighted burrows under the sewers. At every corner the earth threw up blouses and neckties as a volcano throws up lava. It was an intoxicating and a bewildering scene. And presently, in Piccadilly, I saw a large, joyous, expectant, pagan, well-dressed crowd surging at the shut doors of a palace. I wondered whether it could be a theatre, or a remnant sale, or a place where sovereigns were given away. It was a popular restaurant, all marble and gold. The hour was a quarter to six, and the elegance of many suburbs had assembled to compete for its tables. Concerts had filled the afternoon; concerts would divert the evening; and a band was even then playing in the Green Park. This is the city (I said) where the muffin-man used to wander with his mournful tinkles through deserted squares of a Sunday afternoon! This is Spurgeon's city! This is the city which remembered the Sabbath under pain of being banished by an anthropomorphic god to an eternity of fire in the society of an anthropomorphic devil! This is the city where even railway trains dared not move till the benediction had been pronounced.

A great journalist and observer of men said to me: "Yes. They are no longer sure of another life. They aren't convinced now that they can nightly pitch their moving tent a day's march nearer home; and so they establish themselves in Portland stone and pass the time in eating and making music. That is the explanation of our modern luxury and pleasure." But I do not think it is the explanation. At any rate, I think it is only a very small part of the explanation. For example, I know that I, and I know that my friends, had just as much desire for luxury and pleasure twenty years ago as we have now. We could not gratify the taste, simply because the means for gratifying it did not exist. The wealth of the earth had not been sufficiently extracted; invention had not saved enough labour; ways of communication were still barbaric; co-operative organisation had not properly correlated demand and supply; the people had scarcely recovered from their surprise at being able to read, and the popular Press was in its infancy. But was worldly desire unborn? Did the fear of brimstone ever in mundane history stop man from plucking the grapes when he could reach them? The spirit was always the same. Forty years ago, before Matthew Arnold had got himself into a mess by publishing *Literature and Dogma*, before Huxley was respectable, Laurence Oliphant could demand of *his* world, the world which *could* reach the grapes: "Whether Jonah could possibly have had anything to say to Nineveh which would not apply with equal force to this Christian metropolis? – and, if so, what?" It is true that "they" are no longer sure of another life, but I doubt if it is true that "they" are so upset by their sense of insecurity that they feel the need to drown care in champagne. Their attitude is not that of the murderer who on his last morning ordered anchovies for breakfast, though anchovies always disagreed with him.

The fact is that our amazing progress in mechanical invention and in the economic marshalling of industry has occurred simultaneously with a far greater advance, and that the effects of the one are apt to be attributed to the other. They are both symptoms of a general quickening of vitality; but the connection between them is not obvious. Indeed, I should question whether there is a genuine connection between the revival of applied science and the revival of philosophy. Of course, the revival of philosophy is infinitely more important than the revival of science, and equally of course its results are less obvious and slower to come. But they are coming. They are coming. And compared with them the results of science are as naught. Herbert Spencer wrote *First Principles* long before Edison hit on the telephone, and not one man in a thousand who uses a telephone has yet read a line of *First Principles*. But *First Principles* laughs at the Edisonian toy and the man who plays with it, for while he is playing with it *First Principles* has turned a universe upside down, and the man absorbed in the telephone has scarce begun to suspect the revolution. The growth of luxury, the change of manners, are a trifle to what is already close upon us. I was struck, as I passed through a new London, by the extraordinary stridency of the restaurants, nearly all of which were tempting people to indulgence by means of orchestras and singers. But I was far more struck by a long, glaring banner which tempted people to God by the offer of precisely similar attractions. It might have been stretched across the entrance to a penny booth in a fair. It was actually stretched across the portals of St James's Church, Piccadilly – surely the central fastness of British restraint and correctitude. To such a pass had things come! And only yesterday, it seems, the Salvation Army was scorned for the crudity of its drums and trumpets! St James's Church, bravely tearing up its letters to *The Times*, may tell you that it must compete with the restaurants and with the music-halls of the Sunday League. But what it has to compete with is something quite other than the taste for pleasure, something that does not rely on orchestras and singers and banners, and that something is the terrific impetus of the sap of human intelligence and curiosity; it is the revolutionary force of life itself.

We read of the Renaissance as we read of a railway accident, hardly perceiving that it was a real event that happened to real men, and not guessing that it might happen to us. There is a jarring scrunch, a clap of thunder, and we are flung violently into the opposite cushions. But only by degrees do we realise that we are in a railway accident – the sort of thing that is described with awful details in the newspapers. Long afterwards we say, "That was a railway accident!" And our conceptions of a railway accident are for ever altered. In the same way, we are entering now on a mighty change, on a world-movement, on a subversive, vitalizing epoch, compared to which, in my opinion, the Renaissance and the Reformation are insignificant. And long afterwards people will say, "Ah! what a time was that!" But we do not realise it. We shall not realise it fully till all is over. Yet I think we feel that the great storm of life is rising, the clouds gathering, the winds moaning ere they scream. I think that some of us see that luxury and pleasure are nothing but the "white horses" flecking the ocean. It is going to be the greatest storm that that ocean has ever witnessed. Nobody knows, not even the wisest, what will be the end of it – what craft will founder and what will ride the gale. It may, nevertheless, be positively said that those will stand the best chance who put out to sea, the open sea, and rejoice openly in the tempest, accepting it, braving it, and trusting it. And those will stand the worst chance who obstinately pretend that there isn't a storm, or that it will blow over quickly, and who lay up in a cove and drop anchors.

I wonder whether we shall try to do this in England. I rather fear we shall. If we do it will be a pity. Physically courageous, morally courageous, too, in the field of intellectual curiosity we are the most miserable of cowards. We hate to think. We hate those who make us think. Only within the last year or two has "freethinker" ceased to be a word of the direst opprobrium. We have the horrors when we suspect that things will not always be what they were. We have always pretended even that they are not what they are, and any clever fellow who will assist us in the pretence is sure of at least a knighthood. Take our big popular magazines. There is not one which is not armour-clad against any invasion of original thinking, any attack on the great pretence. No popular magazine dares to print a story with an unhappy ending, nor to deal with any open question of theology, philosophy, or politics. We will not have it. We use the term "American" in disdain, but American popular magazines are allowed to handle life without gloves, and to come to grips with matters that involve sincere thinking and intellectual courage. There is one which will not merely print a sad, true story, but will pay the author twopence-halfpenny a word for it. These are trifles. How have we treated our great pioneers of thought? There is no copyright in *An Essay on the Principle of Population*, a book universally recognised by competent authority as one of the landmarks of human thought. Is it in Everyman's Library? Is it in the Universal Library? Is it in the World's Classics? Is it in the National Library?

No. Only one publisher in England to-day dares print it. Why? The answer is disgraceful to us. Malthus, the blameless curate of genius, whose shade must be philosophically startled at our treatment of him, was the first of the real moderns. And he is ours. But the creators of the whole fabric of evolution, of all the thought which has made our intellectual world, are ours too. Herbert Spencer, Alfred Russel Wallace, and Charles Darwin! Fortunately for his reputation with us, Darwin confined himself to masterly physical generalisations; but we still have our knife in him. In a competition for esteem Dickens would leave him out of sight. When Spencer died, a few simple, deluded souls had the strange idea of getting up a memorial to the intelligence who outside England is regarded as supreme. We soon put a stop to that. We laughed hugely at his autobiography. As for Alfred Russel Wallace, he is still with us. Less than a month ago a newspaper was smiling at him as a harmless sort of a lunatic. So we treat the men who force us to think.

I do not want to belittle the English character. I have known other races intimately, and the more I see of other races the more

I admire my own. This is a mature and utterly un-Chauvinistic judgment. But the time is at hand when our terrible national shortcoming, our intellectual poltroonery, bastard of hypocrisy and sentimentalism, may bring us to open shame in the whole world's eye. The stress is upon us, the stress caused by secret and inexplicable forces, of which our taste for luxury and pleasure is simply a minor phenomenon. The storm of life is rising. The Latin nations, with all their sins upon them, will go out into it. The Teutonic nations, with not a tithe of our original brain power, will go out into it. Shall we, a nation of mariners, hide miserably in harbours and pretend that the sky is clear? I do not predict the issue of the storm, but I can surmise the fate of anchored vessels.

Marriage

It has been said by friends, acquaintances, and biographers that Bennett was a sexually repressed man. His marriage to Marguerite Soulié in July 1907 went slowly to pieces, and they separated in 1921, in consequence of her attention to a younger man. His second marriage, to Dorothy Cheston, was marred by considerable unhappiness on her part. Bennett is sometimes quoted against himself on the point. In his *Journal* on 25 May 1908 he wrote: "I see that at bottom, I have an intellectual scorn, or the scorn of an intellectual man, for all sexual-physical manifestations. They seem childish to me, unnecessary symptoms and symbols of a spiritual phenomenon." It is something to be reckoned with, though, that a high proportion of his novels are primarily concerned with women – *The Old Wives' Tale* being the most notable example and *The Pretty Lady* the most sexual; and also that in the years up to his first marriage the *Journal* alludes very often to frank discussion of sex and marriage with both men and women. The *Journal* is reticent in reporting details of such conversations, but it gives no sense of a man who was uninterested in or uneasy about sex. The entry that mentions his intellectual scorn for physical manifestations of the spiritual goes on to say: "Yet few Englishmen could be more perversely curious and adventurous in just these manifestations." In another entry, on 8 July 1904, which tells of a conversation with a young man about celibacy among dons and fellows at Oxford and Cambridge, he notes asking the young man: "Don't you think women are the most interesting thing in the world?" The difference between Bennett and someone like his friend H. G. Wells (who was one of the people to say that Bennett was repressed) was that Bennett practised virtues of loyalty, fidelity, compassion, discretion, and restraint to a degree that was beyond Wells's comprehension or emulation.

Bennett was forty years old when he married Marguerite. He had known her for six months, and had been nursed back to health by her after an illness. Before he proposed, he consulted friends, and they recommended marriage. The following two articles are impersonal discussions of marriage written for the "Savoir-Vivre Papers" in *T.P.'s Weekly*. Their special interest is that they were written six months after his marriage. They appeared on 2 and 9 February 1908, and were reprinted in *Mental Efficiency* in 1912.

The Two Ways of Marriage

Sabine and other summary methods of marrying being now abandoned by all nice people, there remain two broad general ways. The first is the English way. We let nature take her course. We give heed to the heart's cry. When, amid the hazards and accidents of the world, two souls "find each other", we rejoice. Our instinctive wish is that they shall marry, if the matter can anyhow be arranged. We frankly recognise the claim of romance in life, and we are prepared to make sacrifices to it. We see a young couple at the altar; they are in love. Good! They are poor. So much the worse! But nevertheless we feel that love will pull them through. The revolting French system of bargain and barter is the one thing that we can neither comprehend nor pardon in the customs of our great neighbours. We endeavour to be polite about that system; we simply cannot. It shocks our finest, tenderest feelings. It is so obviously contrary to nature.

The second is the French way, just alluded to as bargain and barter. Now, if there is one thing a Frenchman can neither comprehend nor pardon in the customs of a race so marvellously practical and sagacious as ourselves, it is the English marriage system. He endeavours to be polite about it, and he succeeds. But it shocks his finest, tenderest feelings. He admits that it is in accordance with nature; but he is apt to argue that the whole progress of civilisation has been the result of an effort to get away from nature. "What! Leave the most important relation into which a man can enter to the mercy of chance, when a mere gesture may arouse passion, or the colour of a corsage induce desire! No, you English, you who are so self-controlled, you are not going seriously to defend that! You talk of love as though it lasted for ever. You talk of sacrificing to love; but what you really sacrifice, or risk sacrificing, is the whole of the latter part of married existence for the sake of the first two or three years. Marriage is not one long honeymoon. We wish it were. When *you* agree to a marriage you fix your eyes on the honeymoon. When *we* agree to a marriage we try to see it as it will be five or ten years hence. We assert that, in the average instance, five years after the wedding it doesn't matter whether the parties were in love or not on the wedding-day. Hence we will not yield to the gusts of the moment. Your system is, moreover, if we may be permitted the observation, a premium on improvidence; it is, to some extent, the result of improvidence. You can marry your daughters without dowries, and the ability to do so tempts you to neglect your plain duty to your daughters, and you do not always resist the temptation. Do your marriages of 'romance' turn out better than our marriages of prudence, of careful thought, of long foresight? We do not think they do."

So much for the two ways. Patriotism being the last refuge of a scoundrel, according to Doctor Johnson, I have no intention of judging between them, as my heart prompts me to do, lest I should be accused of it. Nevertheless, I may hint that, while perfectly convinced by the admirable logic of the French, I am still, with the charming illogicalness of the English, in favour of romantic marriages (it being, of course, understood that dowries *ought* to be far more plentiful than they are in England). If a Frenchman accuses me of being ready to risk sacrificing the whole of the latter part of married life for the sake of the first two or three years, I would unhesitatingly reply: "Yes, I *am* ready to risk that sacrifice. I reckon the first two or three years are worth it." But, then, I am English, and therefore romantic by nature. Look at London, that city whose outstanding quality is its romantic quality; and look at the Englishwomen going their ways in the wonderful streets thereof! Their very eyes are full of romance. They may, they do, lack *chic*, but they are heroines of drama. Then look at Paris; there is little romance in the fine right lines of Paris. Look at the Parisiennes. They are the most astounding and adorable women yet invented by nature. But they aren't romantic, you know. They don't know what romance is. They are so matter-of-fact that when you think of their matter-of-factness it gives you a shiver in the small of your back.

To return. One may view the two ways in another light. Perhaps the difference between them is, fundamentally, less a difference between the ideas of two races than a difference between the ideas of two "times of life"; and in France the elderly attitude predominates. As people get on in years, even English people, they are more and more in favour of the marriage of reason as against the marriage of romance. Young people, even French people, object strongly to the theory and practice of the marriage of reason. But with them the unique and precious ecstasy of youth is not past, whereas their elders have forgotten its savour. Which is right? No one will ever be able to decide. But neither the one system nor the other will apply itself well to all or nearly all cases. There have been thousands of romantic marriages in England of which it may be said that it would have been better had the French system been in force to prevent their existence. And, equally, thousands of possible romantic marriages have been prevented in France which, had the English system prevailed there, would have turned out excellently. The prevalence of dowries in England would not render the English system perfect (for it must be remembered that money is only one of several ingredients in the French marriage), but it would considerably improve it. However, we are not a provident race, and we are not likely to become one. So our young men must reconcile themselves to the continued absence of dowries.

The reader may be excused for imagining that I am at the end of my remarks. I am not. All that precedes is a mere preliminary to what follows. I want to regard the case of the man who has given the English system a fair trial and found it futile. Thus, we wait on chance in England. We wait for love to arrive. Suppose it doesn't arrive? Where is the English system then? Assume that a man in a position to marry reaches thirty-five or forty without having fallen in love. Why should he not try the French system for a change? As I have said in other words in a previous article, any marriage is better than none at all. Naturally, in England, he couldn't go up to the Chosen Fair and announce: "I am not precisely in love with you, but will you marry me?" He would put it differently. And she would understand. And do you think she would refuse? I don't.

The Adventure of Marriage

I now proceed to the individual case of the man who is "in a position to marry" and whose affections are not employed. Of course, if he has fallen in love, unless he happens to be a person of extremely powerful will, he will not weigh the pros and cons of marriage; he will merely marry, and forty thousand cons will not prevent him. And he will be absolutely right and justified, just as the straw as it rushes down the current is absolutely right and justified. But the privilege of falling in love is not given to everybody, and the inestimable privilege of falling deeply in love is given to few. However, the man whom circumstances permit to marry but who is not in love, or is only slightly amorous, will still think of marriage. How will he think of it?

I will tell you. In the first place, if he has reached the age of thirty unscathed by Aphrodite, he will reflect that that peculiar feeling of romantic expectation with which he gets up every morning would cease to exist after marriage – and it is a highly agreeable feeling! In its stead, in moments of depression, he would have the feeling of having done something irremediable, of having definitely closed an avenue for the outlet of his individuality. (Kindly remember that I am not describing what this human man ought to think. I am describing what he does think.)

In the second place, he will reflect that, after marriage, he could no longer expect the charming welcomes which bachelors so often receive from women; he would be "done with" as a possibility, and he does not relish the prospect of being done with as a possibility. Such considerations, all connected more or less with the loss of "freedom" (oh, mysterious and thrilling word!), will affect his theoretical attitude. And be it known that even the freedom to be lonely and melancholy is still freedom.

Other ideas will suggest themselves. One morning while brushing his hair he will see a grey hair, and, however young he may be, the anticipation of old age will come to him. A solitary old age! A senility dependent for its social and domestic requirements on condescending nephews and nieces, or even more distant relations! Awful! Unthinkable! And his first movement, especially if he has read that terrible novel, *Fort comme la Mort,* of de Maupassant, is to rush out into the street and propose to the first girl he encounters, in order to avoid this dreadful nightmare of a solitary old age. But before he has got as far as the doorstep he reflects further. Suppose he marries, and after twenty years his wife dies and leaves him a widower! He will still have a solitary old age, and a vastly more tragical one than if he had remained single. Marriage is not, therefore, a sure remedy for a solitary old age; it may intensify the evil. Children? But suppose he doesn't have any children! Suppose, there being children, they die – what anguish! Suppose merely that they are seriously ill and recover – what an ageing experience! Suppose they prove a disappointment – what endless regret! Suppose they "turn out badly" (children do) – what shame! Suppose he finally becomes dependent upon the grudging kindness of an ungrateful child – what a supreme humiliation! All these things are occurring constantly everywhere. Suppose his wife, having loved him, ceased to love him, or suppose he ceased to love his wife! *Ces choses ne se commandent pas* – these things do not command themselves. Personally, I should estimate that in not one per cent even of romantic marriages are the husband and wife capable of *passion* for each other after three years. So brief is the violence of love! In perhaps thirty-three per cent passion settles down into a tranquil affection – which is ideal. In fifty per cent it sinks into sheer indifference, and one becomes used to one's wife or one's husband as to one's other habits. And in the remaining sixteen per cent it develops into dislike or detestation. Do you think my percentages are wrong, you who have been married a long time and know what the world is? Well, you may modify them a little – you won't want to modify them much.

The risk of finding one's self ultimately among the sixteen per cent can be avoided by the simple expedient of not marrying. And by the same expedient the other risks can be avoided, together with yet others that I have not mentioned. It is entirely obvious, then (in fact, I beg pardon for mentioning it), that the attitude towards marriage of the heart-free bachelor must be at best a highly cautious attitude. He knows he is already in the frying-pan (none knows better), but, considering the propinquity of the fire, he doubts whether he had not better stay where he is. His life will be calmer, more like that of a hibernating snake; his sensibilities will be dulled; but the chances of poignant suffering will be very materially reduced.

So that the bachelor in a position to marry but not in love will assuredly decide in theory against marriage – that is to say, if he is timid, if he prefers frying-pans, if he is lacking in initiative, if he has the soul of a rat, if he wants to live as little as possible, if he hates his kind, if his egoism is of the miserable sort that dares not mingle with another's. But if he has been more happily gifted he will decide that the magnificent adventure is worth plunging into; the ineradicable and fine gambling instinct in him will urge him to take, at the first chance, a ticket in the only lottery permitted by the British Government. Because, after all, the mutual sense of ownership felt by the normal husband and the normal wife is something unique, something the like of which cannot be obtained without marriage. I saw a man and a woman at a sale the other day; I was too far off to hear them, but I could perceive that they were having a most lively argument – perhaps it was only about initials on pillowcases; they were *absorbed* in themselves; the world did not exist for them. And I thought: "What miraculous exquisite Force is it that brings together that strange, sombre, laconic organism in a silk hat and a loose, black overcoat, and that strange, bright, vivacious, querulous, irrational organism in brilliant fur and feathers?" And when they moved away the most interesting phenomenon in the universe moved away. And I thought: "Just as no beer is bad, but some beer is better than other beer, so no marriage is bad." The chief reward of marriage is something which marriage is bound to give – companionship whose mysterious *interestingness* nothing can stale. A man may hate his wife so that she can't thread a needle without annoying him, but when he dies, or she dies, he can say: "Well, I *was* interested." And one always is. Said a bachelor of forty-six to me the other night: "Anything is better than the void."

The Gate of the Empire

Bennett and Marguerite came to England on 4
December 1907 to stay for three months. He had just
finished Book I of *The Old Wives' Tale,* and he now laid
it aside and wrote his comic novel *Buried Alive.* The
following essay was one of a small group of essays
written for the *Manchester Daily Despatch.* It appeared
on 11 January 1908, and was reprinted in *Paris
Nights.* The images of England in the opening two
paragraphs are akin to those Bennett used in the
closing paragraphs of *The Glimpse,* written in 1909.

❧ ❧ ❧

When one comes back to it, after long absence, one sees exactly
the same staring, cold white cliffs under the same stars. Ministries
may have fallen; the salaries of music-hall artistes may have risen;
Christmas boxes may have become a crime; old-age pensions and
war balloons may be in the air; Home Rule may be underground;
the strange notion may have sprouted that school children must
be fed before they are taught: but all these things are as nothing
compared to the changeless fact of the island itself. You in the
island are apt to forget that the sea is eternally beating round about
all the political fuss you make; you are apt to forget that your
40-h.p. cars are rushing to and fro on a mere whale's back
insecurely anchored in the Atlantic. You may call the Atlantic by
soft, reassuring names, such as Irish Sea, North Sea, and silver

streak; it remains the Atlantic, very careless of social progress, very rude.

The ship under the stars swirls shaking over the starlit waves, and then bumps up against granite and wood, and amid cries ropes are thrown out, and so one is lashed to the island. Scarcely any reasonable harbours in this island! The inhabitants are obliged to throw stones into the sea till they emerge like a geometrical reef, and vessels cling hard to the reef. One climbs on to it from the steamer; it is very long and thin, like a sword, and between shouting wind and water one precariously balances oneself on it. After some eighty years of steam, nothing more comfortable than the reef has yet been achieved. But far out on the water a black line may be discerned, with the silhouettes of cranes and terrific engines. Denied a natural harbour, the island has at length determined to have an unnatural harbour at this bleak and perilous spot. In another ten years or so the peaceful invader will no longer be compelled to fight with a real train for standing room on a storm-swept reef.

❖   ❖   ❖

And that train! Electric light, corridors, lavatories, and general brilliance! Luxuries inconceivable in the past! But, just to prove a robust conservatism, hot-water bottles remain as the sole protection against being frozen to death.

"Can I get you a seat, sir?"

It is the guard's tone that is the very essence of England. You may say he descries a shilling on the horizon. I don't care. That tone cannot be heard outside England. It is an honest tone, cheerful, kindly, the welling-up of a fundamental good nature. It is a tone which says: "I am a decent fellow, so are you; let us do the best for ourselves under difficulties." It is far more English than a beefsteak or a ground-landlord. It touches the returned exile profoundly, especially at the dreadful hour of four a.m. And in replying, "Yes, please. Second. Not a smoker", one is saying, "Hail! Fellow-islander. You have appalling faults, but for sheer straightness you cannot be matched elsewhere."

One comes to an oblong aperture on the reef, something resembling the aperture of a Punch and Judy show, and not much larger. In this aperture are a man, many thick cups, several urns, and some chunks of bread. One struggles up to the man.

"Tea or coffee, sir?"

"Hot milk," one says.

"Hot milk!" he repeats. You have shocked his Toryism. You have dragged him out of the rut of tea and coffee, and he does not like it. However – brave, resourceful fellow – he pulls himself together for an immense effort, and gives you hot milk, and you stand there, in front of the aperture, under the stars and over the sea and in the blast, trying to keep the cup upright in a melee of elbows.

This is the gate, and this the hospitality, of the greatest empire that, etc.

"Can I take this cup to the train?"

"Certainly, sir!" says the Punch and Judy man genially, as who should say: "God bless my soul! Aren't you in the country where anyone can choose the portmanteau that suits him out of a luggage van?"

Now that is England! In France, Germany, Italy, there would have been a spacious golden café and all the drinks on earth, but one could never have got that cup out of the café without at least a stamped declaration signed by two commissioners of police and countersigned by a Consul. One makes a line of milk along the reef, and sits blowing and sipping what is left of the milk in the train. And when the train is ready to depart one demands of a porter:

"What am I to do with this cup?"

"Give it to me, sir."

And he planks it down on the platform next a pillar, and leaves it. And off one goes. The adventures of that thick mug are a beautiful demonstration that the new England contains a lot of the old. It will ultimately reach the Punch and Judy show once more (not broken – perhaps cracked); not, however, by rules and regulations; but higgledy-piggledy, by mutual aid and good nature and good will. Be tranquil; it will regain its counter.

❖   ❖   ❖

The fringe of villas, each primly asleep in its starlit garden, which borders the island and divides the hopfields from the Atlantic, is much wider than it used to be. But in the fields time has stood still. . . . Now, one has left the sea and the storm and the reef, and already one is forgetting that the island is an island. . . . Warmth gradually creeps up from the hot-water bottles to one's heart and eyes, and sleep comes as the train scurries into the empire. . . . A loud reverberation, and one wakes up in a vast cavern, dimly lit, and sparsely peopled by a few brass-buttoned beings that have the air of dwarfs under its high, invisible roof. They give it a name, and call it Charing Cross, and one remembers that, since one last saw it, it fell down and demolished a theatre. Everything is shuttered in the cavern. Nothing to eat or drink, or to read, but shutters. And shutters are so cold, and caverns so draughty.

"Where can I get something to eat?" one demands.

"Eat, sir?" A staggered pause, and the porter looks at one as if one were Oliver Twist. "There's the hotels, sir," he says, finally.

Yet one has not come by a special, unique train, unexpected and startling. No! That train knocks at the inner door of the empire every morning in every month in every year at the same hour, and it is always met by shutters. And the empire, by the fact of its accredited representatives in brass buttons and socialistic ties, is always taken aback by the desire of the peaceful invader to eat.

❖   ❖   ❖

One wanders out into the frozen silence. Gas lamps patiently burning over acres of beautiful creosoted wood! A dead cab or so! A policeman! Shutters everywhere: Nothing else. No change here.

This is the changeless, ineffable Strand at Charing Cross, sacred as the Ganges. One cannot see a single new building. Yet they say London has been rebuilt.

The door of the hotel is locked. And the night watchman opens with the same air of astonishment as the Punch and Judy man when one asked for milk, and the railway porter when one asked for food. Every morning at that hour the train stops within fifty yards of the hotel door, and pitches out into London persons who have been up all night; and London blandly continues to be amazed at their arrival. A good English fellow, the watchman – almost certainly the elder brother of the train-guard.

"I want a room and some breakfast."

He cautiously relocks the door.

"Yes, sir, as soon as the waiters are down. In about an hour, sir. I can take you to the lavatory now, sir, if that will do."

Who said there was a new England?

One sits overlooking the Strand, and tragically waiting. And presently, in the beginnings of the dawn, that pathetic, wistful object the first omnibus of the day rolls along – all by itself – no horses in front of it! And, after hours, a waiter descends as bright as a pin from his attic, and asks with a strong German accent whether one will have tea or coffee. The empire is waking up, and one is in the heart of it.

Industry

The following article appeared in the *Manchester Daily Despatch* on 17 February 1908, and was reprinted in *Paris Nights*. The opening remarks on the Englishness of the Potteries recall similar remarks in the opening of *The Old Wives' Tale*; the closing remarks on ignorance and culture recall the fine story "The Death of Simon Fuge" that Bennett wrote in 1907.

☽❦ ☽❦ ☽❦

My native heath, thanks to the enterprise of London newspapers and the indestructibility of picturesque lies, has the reputation of being quite unlike the rest of England, but when I set foot in it after absence, it seems to me the most English piece of England that I ever came across. With extraordinary clearness I see it as absurdly, ridiculously, splendidly English. All the English characteristics are, quite remarkably, exaggerated in the Potteries. (That is perhaps why it is a butt for the organs of London civilisation.) This intensifying of a type is due no doubt to a certain isolation, caused partly by geography and partly by the inspired genius of the gentleman who, in planning what is now the London and North-Western Railway, carefully diverted it from a populous district and sent it through a hamlet six miles away. On the 28 miles between Stafford and Crewe of the four-track way of the greatest line in England, not a town! And a solid population of a quarter of a million within gunshot! English methods! That is to say, the preposterous side of English methods.

We practise in the Potteries the fine old English plan of not calling things by their names. We are one town, one unseparated mass of streets. We are, in fact, the twelfth largest town in the United Kingdom (though you would never guess it). And the chief of our retail commerce and of our amusements are congregated in the centre of our town, as the custom is. But do not imagine that we will consent to call ourselves one town. No! We pretend that we are six towns, and to carry out the pretence we have six town halls, six Mayors or chief bailiffs, six sanitary inspectors, six everything, including six jealousies. We find it so much more economical, convenient, and dignified, in dealing with public health, education, and railway, canal, and tramway companies to act by means of six mutually jealous authorities.

❖   ❖   ❖

We make your cups and saucers – and other earthen utensils. We have been making them for over a thousand years. And, since we are English, we want to make them now as we made them a thousand years ago. We flatter ourselves that we are a particularly hard-headed race, and we are. Steel drills would not get a new idea into our hard heads. We have a characteristic shrewd look, a sort of looking askance and suspicious. We are looking askance and suspicious at the insidious approaches of science and scientific organisation. At the present moment the twelfth largest town is proposing to find a sum of £250 (less than it spends on amusement in a single day) towards the cost of a central school of pottery. Mind, only proposing! Up to three years ago (as has been publicly stated by a master-potter) we carped at scientific methods. "Carp" is an amiable word. We hated and loathed innovation. We do still. Only a scientific, adventurous, un-English manufacturer who has dared to innovate knows the depth and height, the terrific inertia, of that hate and that loathing.

Oh, yes, we are fully aware of Germany! Yesterday a successful manufacturer said to me – and these are his exact words, which I wrote down and read over to him: "Owing to superior technical knowledge, the general body of German manufacturers are able to produce certain effects in china and in earthenware, which the general body of English manufacturers are incapable of producing." However, we have already established two outlying minor technical schools, and we are proposing to find £250 privately towards a grand and imposing central technical college. Do not smile, you who read this. You are not arch-angels, either. Besides, when we like, we can produce the finest earthenware in the world. We are only just a tiny bit more English than you – that's all. And the Potteries is English industry in little – a glass for English manufacture to see itself in.

❖   ❖   ❖

For the rest, we are the typical industrial community, presenting the typical phenomena of new England. We have made municipal parks out of wildernesses, and hired brass bands of music to play in them. We have quite six parks in our town. The character of our annual carnivals has improved out of recognition within living memory. Electricity no longer astounds us. We have public baths everywhere (though I have never heard that they rival our gasworks in contributing to the rates). Our public libraries are better and more numerous, though their chief function is still to fleet the idle hours of our daughters. Our roads are less awful. Our slums are decreasing. Our building regulations are stricter. Our sanitation is vastly improved; and in spite of asthma, lead-poisoning, and infant mortality our death-rate is midway between those of Manchester and Liverpool.

We grow steadily less drunken. Yet drunkenness remains our worst vice, and in the social hierarchy none stands higher than the brewer, precisely as in the rest of England. We grow steadily less drunken, but even the intellectuals still think it odd and cranky to meet without drinking fluids admittedly harmful; and as for the workingman's beer. . . . Knock the glass out of his hand and see! We grow steadily less drunken, but we possess some 750 licensed houses and not a single proper bookshop. No man could make a hundred pounds a year by selling books in the Potteries. We really do not know a lot, and we have as many bathrooms per thousand as any industrial hive in this island, and as many advertisements of incomparable soaps. We are in the way of perfection, and when we have conquered drunkenness, ignorance, and dirt we shall have arrived there, with the rest of England. Dirt – a public slatternliness, a public and shameless flouting of the virtues of cleanliness and tidiness – is the most spectacular of our sins.

We are the supreme land of picturesque contrasts. On one day last week I saw a Town Clerk who had never heard of H. G. Wells; I walked five hundred yards and assisted at a performance of chamber-music by Bach and a discussion of the French slang of Huysmans; walked only another hundred yards and was, literally, stuck in an unprotected bog and extricated therefrom by the kindness of two girls who were rooting in a shawdruck for bits of coal.

Lastly, with other industrial communities, we share the finest of all qualities – the power and the will to work. We do work. All of us work. We have no use for idlers. Climb a hill and survey our combined endeavour, and you will admit it to be magnificent.

The Hanbridge Empire

In the Five Towns novels Hanley was Hanbridge, and the Grand Theatre of Varieties was the Hanbridge Empire. Bennett visited the Five Towns in December 1909 as part of his preparation for writing the *Clayhanger* trilogy. On the 8th he wrote in his *Journal*: "After dinner I went to the Grand Theatre, 9:15 p.m. I was profoundly struck by all sorts of things. In particular by the significance of clog-dancing, which had never occurred to me before. . . . I . . . got into an extraordinary vein of 'second sight'. I perceived whole chapters." In *Clayhanger* Florence Simcox dances in clogs, and sets young Edwin dreaming.

"The Hanbridge Empire" appeared in the *Nation* on 11 June 1910, and was reprinted in *Paris Nights*.

When I came into the palace, out of the streets where black human silhouettes moved on seemingly mysterious errands in the haze of high-hung electric globes, I was met at the inner portal by the word "Welcome" in large gold letters. This greeting, I saw, was part of the elaborate mechanics of the place. It reiterated its message monotonously to perhaps fifteen thousand visitors a week; nevertheless, it had a certain effectiveness, since it showed that the Hanbridge Theatres Company Limited was striving after the right attitude towards the weekly fifteen thousand. At some pit doors the seekers after pleasure are received and herded as if they were criminals, or beggars. I entered with curiosity, for, though it is the business of my life to keep an eye on the enthralling social phenomena of Hanbridge, I had never been in its Empire. When I formed part of Hanbridge there was no Empire; nothing but sing-songs conducted by convivial chairmen with rapping hammers in public-houses whose blinds were drawn and whose posters were in manuscript. Not that I have ever assisted at one of those extinct sing-songs. They were as forbidden to me as a High Church service. The only convivial rapping chairman I ever beheld was at Gatti's, under Charing Cross Station, twenty-two years ago.

Now I saw an immense carved and gilded interior, not as large as the Paris Opera, but assuredly capable of seating as many persons. My first thought was: "Why, it's just like a real music hall!" I was so accustomed to regard Hanbridge as a place where the great visible people went in to work at seven a.m. and emerged out of public houses at eleven p.m., or stood movelessly mournful in packed tramcars, or bitterly partisan on chill football grounds, that I could scarcely credit their presence here, lolling on velvet amid gold Cupids and Hercules, and smoking at ease, with plentiful ash-trays to encourage them. I glanced round to find acquaintances, and the first I saw was the human being who nine to seven was my tailor's assistant; not now an automaton wound up with deferential replies to any conceivable question that a dandy could put, but a living soul with a calabash between his teeth, as fine as anybody. Indeed, finer than most! He, like me, reclined aristocratic in the grand circle (a bob). He, like me, was offered chocolates and what not at reasonable prices by a boy whose dress indicated that his education was proceeding at Eton. I was glad to see him. I should have gone and spoken to him, only I feared that by so doing I might balefully kill a man and create a deferential automaton. And I was glad to see the vast gallery with human twopences. In nearly all public places of pleasure, the pleasure is poisoned for me by the obsession that I owe it, at last, to the underpaid labour of people who aren't there and can't be there; by the growing, deepening obsession that the whole structure of what a respectable person means, when he says with patriotic warmth "England", is reared on a stupendous and shocking injustice. I did not feel this at the Hanbridge Empire.

Even the newspaper-lad and the match-girl might go to the Hanbridge Empire and, sitting together, drink the milk of paradise. Wonderful discoverers, these new music-hall directors all up and down the United Kingdom! They have discovered the folk.

    ✦   ✦   ✦

The performance was timed as carefully as a prize-fight. Ting! and the curtain went unfailingly up. Ting! and it came unfailingly down. Ting! and something started. Ting! and it stopped. Everybody concerned in the show knew what he and everybody else had to do. The illuminated number-signs on either side of the proscenium changed themselves with the implacable accuracy of astronomical phenomena. It was as though some deity of ten thousand syndicated halls was controlling the show from some throne studded with electric switches in Shaftesbury Avenue. Only the uniformed shepherd of the twopences aloft seemed free to use his own discretion. His "Now then, order, *please*", a masterly union of entreaty and intimidation, was the sole feature of the entertainment not regulated to the fifth of a second by that recurrent ting.

But what the entertainment gained in efficient exactitude by this ruthless ordering, it seemed to lose in zest, in capriciousness, in rude joy. It was watched almost dully, and certainly there was nothing in it that could rouse the wayward animal that is in all of us. It was marked by an impeccable propriety. In the classic halls of London you can still hear skittish grandmothers, stars of a past age unreformed, prattling (with an amazing imitation of youthfulness) of champagne suppers. But not in the Hanbridge Empire. At the Hanbridge Empire the curtain never rises on any disclosure of the carnal core of things. Even when a young woman in a short skirt chanted of being clasped in his arms again, the tepid primness of her manner indicated that the embrace would be that of a tailor's dummy and a pretty head-and-shoulders in a hairdresser's window. The pulse never asserted itself. Only in the unconscious but overpowering temperament of a couple of acrobatic mulatto women was there the least trace of bodily fever. Male acrobats of the highest class, whose feats were a continual creation of sheer animal beauty, roused no adequate enthusiasm.

"When do the Yorkshire Songsters come on?" I asked an attendant at the interval. In the bar, a handful of pleasure-seekers were dispassionately drinking, without a rollicking word to mar the flow of their secret reflections.

"Second item in the second part," said the attendant, and added heartily: "And very good they are, too, sir!"

He meant it. He would not have said as much of a man whom in the lounge of a London hotel I saw playing the fiddle and the piano simultaneously. He was an attendant of mature and difficult judgment, not to be carried away by clowning or grotesquerie. With him good meant good. And they were very good. And they were what they pretended to be. There were about twenty of them; the women were dressed in white, and the men wore scarlet hunting coats. The conductor, a little shrewd man, was disguised in a sort of *levée* dress, with knee-breeches and silk stockings. But he could not disguise himself from me. I had seen him, and hundreds of him, in the streets of Halifax, Wakefield, and Batley. I had seen him all over Yorkshire, Lancashire, and Staffordshire. He was a Midland type: infernally well satisfied with himself under a crust of quiet modesty; a nice man to chat with on the way to Blackpool, a man who could take a pot of beer respectably and then stop, who could argue ingeniously with heat, and who would stick a shaft into you as he left you, just to let you know that he was not quite so ordinary as he made out to be. They were all like that, in a less degree; women too; those women could cook a Welsh rarebit with any woman, and they wouldn't say all they thought all at once, either.

And there they were ranged in a flattened semi-circle on a music-hall stage. Perhaps they appeared on forty music-hall stages in a year. It had come to that: another case of specialisation. Doubtless they had begun in small choirs, or in the parlours of home, singing for the pleasure of singing, and then acquiring some local renown; and then the little shrewd conductor had had the grand idea of organised professionalism. God bless my soul! The thing was an epic, or ought to be! They really could sing. They really had voices. And they would not "demean" themselves to cheapness. All their eyes said: "This is no music-hall foolery. This is uncompromisingly high-class, and if you don't like it you ought to be ashamed of yourselves!" They sang part-song music, from "Sweet and Low" to a *Lohengrin* chorus. And with a will, with finesse, with a pianissimo over which the endless drone of the electric fan could be clearly distinguished, and a fine, free fortissimo that would have enchanted Wagner! They brought the house down every time. They might have rendered encores till midnight, but for my deity in Shaftesbury Avenue. It was the "folk" themselves giving back to the folk in the form of art the very life of the folk.

❖   ❖   ❖

But the most touching instance of this giving-back was furnished by the lady clog-dancer. Hanbridge used to be the centre of a land of clogs. Hundreds of times I have wakened in winter darkness to the sound of clogs on slushy pavements. And when I think of clogs I think of the knocker-up, and hurried fire-lighting, and tea and thick bread, and the icy draught from the opened front-door, and the factory gates, and the terrible time-keeper therein, and his clock: all the military harshness of industrialism grimly accepted. Few are the clogs now in Hanbridge. The girls wear paper boots, for their health's sake, and I don't know what the men wear. Clogs have nearly gone out of life. But at the Hanbridge Empire they had reappeared in an art highly conventionalised. The old clog-dancing, begun in public-houses, was realistic, and was done by people who the next morning would clatter to work in clogs. But this pretty, simpering girl had never worn a clog seriously. She had never regarded a clog as a cheap and lasting protection against wind and rain, but as a contrivance that you had to dance in. I daresay she rose at eleven a.m. She had a Cockney accent. She would not let her clogs make a noise. She minced in clogs. It was no part of her scheme to lose her breath. And yet I doubt not that she constituted a romantic ideal for the young male twopences, with her clogs that had reached her natty feet from the original back streets of, say, Stockport. As I lumbered home in the electric car, besieged by printed requests from the tram company not on any account to spit, I could not help thinking and thinking, in a very trite way, that art is a wonderful thing.

The People of the Potteries

The several towns of the Potteries were joined in loose federation on 31 March 1910. In *The Old Wives' Tale* the last public act of Constance is to go out in the rain to vote against federation, and federation is defeated. But she catches a chill and dies, and at her funeral the sardonic Charles Critchlow says, "It's a pity her didn't live long enough to hear as Federation is going on after all! That would ha' worritted her." "The People of the Potteries" was published in *Cassell's Magazine* in January 1911.

꙰ꙍ   ꙰ꙍ   ꙰ꙍ

I

The stranger, unless he enters the district by night, cannot be absolutely carried away by his first sight of the Potteries. At night, with its furnace fires leaping upwards amid vast clouds of tinted vapour and smoke, and reflecting themselves in the black water of mysterious canals, the Potteries may claim a beauty and a majesty of its own. But in the daytime its most determined admirer could not call it pretty, or even tidy, and certainly not clean. When the Manchester express sets you down at Stoke-on-Trent Station, which is the traffic centre of the district, you can within five minutes feel the dirt of the Potteries sticking to your skin. You see about you a determined and perhaps (to you) somewhat brusque population, which eyes you with provincial cautiousness, as if to say: "What are you doing here?" You may leave the station and travel through miles and miles and yet miles of streets (chiefly muddy with a black mud), and see nothing but tramcars whizzing up and down between endless buildings obviously not designed by Christopher Wren or Inigo Jones and rearing up behind the buildings ten thousand chimneys, each trying to send black smoke to Paradise – and not succeeding. You will be so preoccupied by the dirt, the noise, the self-centred bustle, and the sordid monotony of the architecture that probably you will miss that glimpse of green which signalises a new municipal park. If you escape from the streets you will fall into huge cinder-wastes, or lose yourself among artificial mountain ranges of mine-refuse; and when you do get a view of a distant horizon, that horizon will surely be crowned by a pithead and a scarf of smoke, and the intervening rural country will have the colour, not of grass, but of dried peas. Struggling back into the streets you will search afresh but in vain for the magnificent thoroughfares, the imposing squares, the noble edifices which mark a city of a quarter of a million inhabitants, which is the total of the Potteries. In the largest of the Pottery towns the town hall looks like a fairly big hotel (and used to be one), whereas a diminutive building that has some resemblance to a town hall (and used to be one) is nothing but a bank and lawyers' offices. And you will find everywhere the same bland spirit of Making-it-do. It is conceivable that in the end you will exclaim in your wrath and your disgust:

"They told me this was the twelfth largest city in the United Kingdom. I came to see it, and I've got nothing for my pains but a coat of dirt, a headache, and a nightmarish impression of chimneys and rows of windows and everlasting smoke. As for the people, they seem a stern race, and they seem to suspect one of some nefarious design. I don't want to hurt your feelings, but—"

Do not be afraid. You will not hurt our feelings. We sympathise with you. We ourselves, the natives, on some wet day of autumn or spring, have stood in our main streets and beheld the foul prospect,

"Where all but man is vile,"

and have said to ourselves: "It is absolutely astounding that we can live in such a spot and enjoy it". Yet we do, unless the weather goes to extremes. We do and the reason is that we understand. You don't understand. Aware that you don't understand, we permit not our feelings to be hurt. Indeed, far from blaming you, we rather have pity for you.

II

To understand the Potteries it is necessary to dip into geology and geography – these two sciences being, in fact, the key to nearly all human history. If you look at a geological map of Staffordshire, you will see at the northern end of this county, amid expanses of brown (which means sandstone) and blue (which means limestone) a solitary little triangular patch of dark grey (which means coal). The Potteries is in the middle of that patch. Geology has set it apart. And if you look at an ordinary map of Staffordshire, you will see that the Potteries is cut off from the rest of England on the north by wild and hilly moorlands, and on the south by the remains of ancient forests. You will see also that there is no navigable river anywhere near it; in brief, it has got lost in the very middle of the island. And if you looked at ancient maps you would see that the roads to it were few, and that in particular Watling Street passed far to the south of it on the way to Chester and far to the north of it on the way to York.

The Potteries is the Potteries because on that precise spot of the surface of the British Empire there were deposits of clay and of quick-burning coal close to the surface. If this was not an invitation on the part of Nature to make pots, what was it? Wherever the clay and the coal were found close together, there a town sprang up. It was only a tiny town, because nine or ten centuries ago the demand for pots was limited and the processes of manufacture primitive. And each tiny town kept itself to itself, because the landscape was hilly and irregular; it was not a smooth plain; and the roads were naught but mule-tracks.

Cut off from the surrounding country in spirit by the peculiarity of its manufacture and in body by the difficulty of access and its wild environment, the Potteries was indeed isolated. It acquired through centuries the habit of solitude. It was an island in an island. And even when, in the eighteenth century, the canals of England were dug, the Potteries had difficulty in connecting itself with the outer world. Newcastle-under-Lyme objected to canals. I have not yet mentioned Newcastle-under-Lyme, which is a very ancient town lying just to the west of the Potteries on a piece of ground where there is a "fault" in the coal-deposits. A clean town, aristocratic! It was sending two members to Parliament in the fourteenth century. The Potteries had to fight hard with its old-fashioned neighbour before it could possess itself of such a new-fashioned convenience as a canal. The same with railways! The main line (now the London and North-Western) that runs from London through Stafford to the north ought to have gone right through the Potteries on its way to Crewe. But it didn't. The stronger influences were against railways, and the line was diverted through fields and villages that had no special need of it. Hence the Potteries had to construct a railway of its own. It did construct a railway of its own, the North Staffordshire, which gradually became so important that the North-Western had to run its expresses over it. And to-day, when you return from your visit, the express will rush you without a stop over the 146 miles between Stoke and Euston in three hours or less. This is travelling! This is a sign of the Great Change!

III

But great changes do not happen suddenly. Now that you understand, you will not be surprised that the architecture of the twelfth largest town is like the architecture of a small town. The Potteries, despite its extent and its numbers, is in origin a scattering of small towns whose tentacles have spread and joined and interlaced. Now that you understand, you will not be surprised that there was so much local opposition to the federation of the small towns into one big one. During centuries each town had been nursing its individuality in the isolated remoteness of its valley or its hill, and one cannot undo the work of seven hundred years in seven. Now that you understand, you will not be surprised that the inhabitants regard you, the obvious stranger, with a preliminary cautiousness. To do so is the profound instinct of withdrawn communities. Nor will you be surprised later, at the extraordinary heartiness of their hospitality. Such hospitality is the profound instinct of withdrawn communities.

And I hope that you will not be surprised at the dirt and the large slatternliness of the district's physiognomy. I hope that you will drop that attitude of disgust and blame which is so foolishly characteristic of the people who come from an agricultural or a bureaucratic community into an industrial one. Ruskin gorgeously inveighed against the spectacular horrors of industrialism. But he would probably have been very cross if he had had to drink his tea out of the hollow of his hand, in default of a cup and to keep himself warm with a skipping-rope, in default of coal. Yet neither cups nor coals can be produced without a great deal of dirt. You use coal; you want coal, you are very glad to have coal and a number of other things which cannot exist without coal; and then you have the audacity to come into a coaly and clayey district and turn up your nose and say: "Really this is very dirty and untidy!"

My good sir, what did you expect? How would you remedy it? Why, you can't even fetch a hundredweight of coal out of the cellar without soiling your lily-white hands! You as much as anybody are responsible for the external look of things in the Potteries. Forswear coal, forswear cups and saucers, and persuade others to do so, and the Potteries will rapidly take on the purity of Tooting Bec.

You observe here, perhaps, a slight heat and vivacity in our demeanour towards you. Well, the fact is that, conscious as we are of our manifold sins, we really do not expect to be blamed for our soot. In the matter of our soot, we expect, from intelligent and benignant persons, a sympathetic comprehension, and no arrogance of reproof. . . . Yes, we are careless of appearances, but this is one of the faults that enforced dirt invariably engenders. And we did not choose our occupations. Geological strata are responsible for our occupations and our little peculiarities.

IV

Evolution in the Potteries has been quite remarkably dramatic during the Victorian and Edwardian eras. And, of course, it has marched with the improvement in the means of communication. Long after the death of Josiah Wedgwood, its supreme hero, the Potteries retained the primitive characteristics of a district cut off by Nature from the rest of the world. Josiah Wedgwood was a great man and did much, but his impress was left far more deeply on the manufacture of pottery than on the habits of the potters. A great-uncle of my own used often to tell me stories of bear and dog fights at which he assisted as a boy. At that time Burslem, the "Mother" of the other towns Hanley, Stoke-on-Trent, Longton, and Tunstall, had its municipal bear, and Sunday was the day of battles. "But what about the law?" I asked him. "Bless ye!" he would reply, "there was no law in the Potteries in those days." The statement was exaggerated, but it had some truth. Hundreds of men still alive in the Potteries can remember a period when, during the annual "wakes", the public-houses kept open day and night for a week, and the sole ambition of the population seemed to be to get drunk and to remain drunk. In my youth the population of the Potteries was at least a hundred and thirty thousand, and the towns were even then merged into one another, and yet there existed less than two miles of tram line in the entire district, and only two trams – drawn by horses and travelling between Hanley and Burslem – twice an hour. Now, electric cars in scores run about everywhere, from Longton in the south to Tunstall in the north, and from Newcastle in the west to Smallthorn in the east.

And it was precisely these rapid cars which at last broke down the stubborn individualism of the separate towns and brought about their federation and the triumph of Hanley, the central and the largest town. Another case of geography influencing history! Hanley was in the middle. These cars were always flying to Hanley; and the large shops and places of amusement were very tempting. And so the large shops and other establishments grew larger and more numerous, and they are still growing and increasing, and Hanley will soon have a population of a hundred thousand. Inevitably the retail trade of the other towns languished. Useless for the other towns to complain! Useless to fight against the temptation of those cars! For a penny or twopence, in a quarter of an hour, the man or woman with money to spend could be in Hanley, and not all his love for his native town would keep that man or woman out of Hanley. Thus a smaller patriotism was gradually over-come by a greater patriotism, and the tendency of the potters to think of themselves as one single community instead of half a dozen different communities was strengthened. And though each town still protests against losing its identity, its identity will undoubtedly have to go. The loss is part of the price paid for progress and for breadth of mind. Even Hanley, the victor, has had to sacrifice something. It would have liked the federated Potteries to be baptised with its own name; but in the struggle for nomenclature, Stoke-on-Trent has won, and rightly, for it is the centre of the railway system and of the postal system. To the outside world of travellers and addressers of envelopes the Potteries has always been associated with Stoke-on-Trent, and the association will properly remain.

V

But this formal federation, this solemn announcement to the rest of Britain that Britain is henceforth adorned with a new city of formidable dimensions, is only the outward sign and crown of the movement that steadily but unfussily has been transforming the Potteries during the last thirty years. All things considered, the Potteries has learnt very quickly its lesson of closer contact with the world. It has not yet shed the whole of its primitive temperament, and in all probability it never will – at any rate I hope not, but its progress has been remarkable. Little by little it has become studded with municipal institutions and organisations of amenity, of all kinds; its public life has quickened and developed activities as complicated as may be found in any of your swagger municipalities. Most important of all, perhaps, it has grown conscious of its own ugliness, and has seriously set about to titivate itself. Municipal parks flourish and blossom now in every quarter of it. There are at least half a dozen. A municipal park may seem to you a very little thing, but I tell you that in a district martyrised by smoke and fumes, a municipal park is a very great thing indeed, an achievement that approaches the heroic. And if you who sniff at our municipal parks could only compare their appearance with the original appearance of the ground which they occupy, you would agree with me. Swards do not grow of their own accord in the Potteries. The municipal gardeners will tell you that each blade of grass has to be brought up, as it were, by hand. And, in the matter of titivation and beautifying, there is now even a movement for abating the smoke nuisance. Just as some years ago a small band of enthusiasts convinced themselves that federation must come, and federation did come, in the teeth of intense instinctive opposition, so now a small band of enthusiasts have convinced themselves that smoke must go. And though the project seems a dream, and though people inured to dirt will cling to dirt, yet I believe that smoke ultimately will go; for it has been proved that earthenware can be fired better by gas than by coal.

VI

The racial character of the potters is just about what a thoughtful person would expect it to be. It is a mixture. The old and the new are mingled in it. It has the downrightness and simplicity of a withdrawn and relatively small community, and also the marked provincial shrewdness and suspiciousness of such a community. It has the energy of its situation and bracing climate. It has the fierceness and the external harshness of a people engaged in hard bodily labour under conditions which are more frequently inclement than soft. It still has that carelessness of appearances which is the inevitable result of enforced trafficking with coal and clay. But on the other hand in no district in the world will you see more advertisements of soap than in the Potteries. The potters look askance out of their secular isolation at new movements and ideals, but when once they have persuaded themselves of the value of such movements, all their passionate force is thrown into them – and things move! Some day the Potteries will awake even to the importance of technical education and the organisation of its staple trade – and then miracles will be seen in the land. That desired day has tarried too long.

A people may be judged by its amusements and diversions. And the Potteries may well allow itself to be so judged. Gone are bear-baiting, cock-fighting, and rabbit-coursing. Even prison-bars have gone – that violent and almost prehistoric game in which the players would throw themselves into canals in order to avoid defeat. Grown men no longer play at marbles, as they used to do when I went to school. Of the more ancient diversions, pigeon-flying alone remains a very harmless hobby. Football now reigns and has no serious rival. The Potteries was one of the first centres of football and in the history of the Association game the name of Stoke-on-Trent is glorious. Football has characteristics of force and violence and spectacular bigness which could not fail to appeal to such a race as the potters. Cricket is much practised, and golf waxes yearly, but there is nothing like football in North Staffordshire. The publication of the Saturday evening Football edition of the *Staffordshire Sentinel,* the great, the wealthy, and the only daily paper in the Potteries, is a weekly event that sends a thrill through the entire population.

"Yes", you say, in your haste, and your facile superiority. "But they don't play football, they pay to see it played." You are quite wrong. This is a notion which you have picked up ready-made from pessimistic opponents of the professionalisation of sport – persons who see the ruin of British manhood in the vision of ten thousand people gathered round a field to watch twenty-two young men knock a ball about with their feet – and with their heads. Football is tremendously played in North Staffordshire, where there are scores, and I dare say hundreds of football clubs as completely unprofessional as the Corinthians themselves. Look at the crowded pages of results in the *Sentinel* on a Saturday night. There could indeed be no professional football without a vast substructure of amateur football. But those watching, idle thousands. Well, if you know anything about football, you must know that it is a game which cannot be played after a certain age. Its demands on the physical frame are too exacting. Few men can play football after thirty, and practically none after thirty-five. Men don't, as a rule, die at thirty-five. At thirty-five they still have the right to amuse themselves. Most of them cannot buy golf balls at a florin apiece, nor pay guinea subscriptions to golf clubs. What then are they to do? Loll gossiping against bars in stuffy interiors, or shout themselves hoarse under the fresh and stimulating smoke of football grounds? Which is better? A vast deal too much nonsense is talked about football.

VII

Nevertheless, let us admit for argument's sake that football is a violent and even a ferocious pastime. Let us admit all the evils that have ever been debited against it. What is the other great outstanding diversion of the Potteries? Well, it happens to be music. There you have the mixture of the Pottery character symbolised: Football and Music!

In the Potteries music is practised in its most genuinely popular form, that of chorus-singing. The people pay to hear, but it is the people also who sing. They are entertained, but they also entertain. Just as North Staffordshire was one of the first centres of football, so it was one of the first centres of really ambitious chorus-singing. The late Josiah Powell, in the intervals of his work as town clerk of the "Mother of the Potteries", found time to be a pioneer of the Tonic Sol-fa movement. He digged and cultivated a fruitful soil, and the choirs which directly or indirectly owe their existence to his enthusiasm are known wherever Eisteddfods and other musical competitions occur. Yea, they are known even in London and at Windsor. The Potteries sings because it is racially musical. It rushes away from the factory gates to the rehearsal room because it does veritably love music. It takes a special train to London, gives a concert there, and comes home again the same night because it knows what it can do. This is the other side of its energy. And this is amateurism at its best. I do not know how many choral associations there may be in the Potteries; but when recently its favourite conductor died, five choirs and ten thousand people attended his funeral.

For the rest, the intellectual elite of the Potteries are not to be distinguished from the intellectual elite of any other district, except, perhaps, by the vivacity with which they express their opinions.

Paris Streets

Bennett moved from 4 rue de Calais to 3 rue d'Aumale in December 1906. In April 1908 he and Marguerite moved into the Villa des Néfliers near Fontainebleau. In October 1910 they took a flat at 59 rue de Grenelle, and in another several months they decided to give up the Villa des Néfliers. The following sketch was the third section of "My Reminiscences", which was published in the *Strand Magazine* and the *Metropolitan Magazine* in 1913.

When from London I look back at Paris, I always see the streets – such as the Rue Notre Dame de Lorette, the Rue des Martyrs, the Rue Fontaine, and the Rue d'Aumale (one of the most truly Parisian streets in Paris) – which lie on the steep slope between the Rue de Chateaudun and the exterior boulevard where Montmarte begins. Though I have lived in various quarters of Paris on both banks of the Seine, it is to these streets that my memory ever returns. And though I have lived for many years in London, no London street makes the same friendly and intimate appeal to me as these simple middle-class streets of little shops and flats over the shops, with little restaurants, little cafés, and little theatres here and there at the corner. The morning life of these streets was delightful, with the hatless women and girls shopping, and the tradesmen – and, above all, the tradeswomen – polite and firm at their counters, and the vast omnibuses scrambling up or thundering down, and the placid customers in the little cafés. The waiters in the cafés and restaurants were human; they are inhuman in London. The *concierges* of both sexes were fiends, but they were human fiends. There was everywhere a strange mixture of French industry (which is tremendous) and French nonchalance (which is charmingly awful). Virtue and wickedness were equally apparent and equally candid. Hypocrisy alone was absent. I could find more intellectual honesty within a mile of the Rue d'Aumale than in the whole of England. And, more than anything whatever, I prize intellectual honesty.

❖   ❖   ❖

And then the glimpses of domestic life in the serried flats, poised story beyond story upon butchers' and grocers' and confectioners' and music-dealers' and repairers' and drapers' and corset-makers' and walking-stick-makers' and "bazaars"! Thousands of half-visible interiors within ten minutes' walk! And the intense mystery that enwrapped one's own house, reposing in the immense discretion of the *concierge* – who, by the way, was not a fiend. I never knew anything about the prodigiously genteel house of which I rented a fragment in the Rue de Calais, except that a retired opera singer lived over my head and a pianoforte professor at the Conservatoire somewhere under my feet. I never saw either of them, but I knew that the ex-opera singer received about a yard of bread every morning and one and a half litres of milk.

❖   ❖   ❖

Every afternoon and sometimes in the evening a distant violin used to play, very badly, six bars – no more – of an air of Verdi's over and over again; never any other tune! The sound was too faint to annoy me, but it was the most melancholy thing that I have ever heard. This phenomenon persisted for years, and I never discovered its origin, though I inquired again and again. Some interior, some existence of an infinite monotonous sadness, was at hand, and yet hidden away from me, inviolate. Whenever I hear that air now I am instantly in Paris, and as near being sentimental as ever I shall be. My ambition had long been to inhabit the Rue d'Aumale – austere, silent, distinguished, icy, and beautiful – and by hazard I did ultimately obtain a flat there, and so left the Rue de Calais. I tell you, I missed the undiscoverable and tragic violin of the Rue de Calais. To this day the souvenir of it will invariably fold me in a delicious spleen. The secret life of cities is a matter for endless brooding.

❖ ❖ ❖

The sole disadvantage of the ability to take an equal delight in town life and in country life is that one is seldom content where one happens to be. Just when I was fully established in my Parisian street I became conscious of a powerful desire to go and live in the French provinces. And I went. I sacrificed my flat and departed – in order to learn about the avarice, the laboriousness, the political independence, and the tranquil charm of the French peasant, and about the scorn which the countryside has for Paris, and about certain rivers and forests of France, and about the high roads and the inns thereon, and what the commercial travellers say to one another of a night in those excellent inns; in short, to understand a little the fabric of the backbone of France. I often desired to be back again in Paris, and, of course, in the end I came back. And then I had the delightful sensation of coming back to the city, not as a stranger, but as one versed in its deviousness. I was able to take up at once the threads which I had dropped, without any of the drudgery and tedium incident to one's first social studies of a foreign capital. I was immediately at home, and I never felt more satisfaction in my citizenship of Paris than at this period. It was also at this period that I carried my Parisianism as far as I am ever likely to carry it.

Railway Accident at Mantes

On 6 July 1911 Bennett went to visit H. G. Wells and his wife at Pont de l'arche. The railway accident described here occurred on the 7th when he was returning to Paris. Six people were injured. On the 8th he made a *Journal* entry about the accident, and also described it in a letter to Mrs Wells. He also described it in his weekly "Books and Persons" article for the *New Age*. Fifteen years later he used it for his novel *Accident*. The sketch here first appeared in the *Cambridge Review* on 22 October 1920, and was reprinted in *Things That Have Interested Me* in 1921. It is the same as the *Journal* entry except that it adds a few lines at the end.

❧ ❧ ❧

There had already been a breakdown in a tunnel. Officials said that a *rotule* of an *attaché* had got broken. It was repaired, and we jolted onwards at, I should say, about 30 to 35 kilometres an hour. Then just after we passed Mantes station there was a really terrific jolting. I knew after four or five jolts that one coach at any rate had left the metals. I was in a sort of large Pulmanesque compartment at the back of the first-class coach, two or three coaches from the engine. The windows broke. The corridor door sailed into the compartment. My stick flew out of the rack. The table smashed itself. I clung hard to the arms of my seat, but fell against an arm-chair in front of me. There was a noise of splintering, and there were various other noises. An old woman lay on the floor crying. I wondered: Shall I remain unharmed until the thing stops? Extreme tension of waiting for the final stoppage! Equilibrium at last, and I was unhurt! I couldn't get out at first. Then someone opened the door. I soothed the old woman. I took my eye-glasses off and put them in their case. I found my hat (under some debris), and my stick. My bag had remained in the rack. I left the train with my belongings, but I had forgotten all about the book I was reading, *L'Eve Future*. This book was all that I lost. Two wounded women were already lying out on the grass at the side of the track. Up above, from the street bordering the cutting, crowds of people were gazing curiously as at a show. One woman asked if she could do anything, and someone said: "A doctor." I walked round to the other side of the train, and a minor official asked me and others to go back, *"Ce n'est pas pour vous commander, mais . . ."* We obeyed. Two coaches lay on their sides. One of them was unwheeled and partly sticking in the ground. No sound came from an overturned second-class coach, though there were people in it. Presently some men began lifting helpless passengers on to cushions which had been laid on the ground. I had no desire of any sort to help. I argued uncompassionately that it was the incompetent railway company's affair. I held my bag and stick and I looked around. I didn't want to see any more wounded nor to be any more *impressioné* than I could help. I had to get to Paris. I certainly didn't observe things very accurately nor take in details well. My recollection of appearances quickly became vague. I remember that the face of one wounded woman was covered with coal-dust. We had shaved a short goods train standing on the next line, and the tender of the train was against our coach. A young American said that it was sticking into our coach, but I don't think that it was. He said that the front part of our coach was entirely telescoped. But it wasn't entirely telescoped. It was, however, all smashed up. My chief impression is of a total wreck brought about in a few seconds.

I walked off up the line towards the station, and met various groups of employees running towards the train. At last two came with a stretcher or ambulance. I passed out of the station into the *place*, and a collector feebly asked me for my ticket, which I didn't give. I went straight to a garage and demanded an auto for Paris.

But all autos had been taken off to the scene of the accident. Having been promised one in due course, I waited some time, and then had a wash and took tea. I couldn't help eating and drinking quickly. Then I was told that two Americans wanted an auto. I said that they might share the one promised to me. Agreed. At last my auto came. The price was 100 francs. A Frenchman came up who wanted to get to Paris quickly (he had not been in the accident). I gave him a place for 20 francs, making a mistake in dividing 100 by 4. This detail shows how I really was under my superficial calmness. We went off at 5.50. The two Americans, aunt and nephew, chatted freely the whole time, with no sign of nerves, except that the aunt said she never felt comfortable in an auto. Nothing had happened to her, yet the gunmetal clasp of her handbag was all bent. She discovered this in the auto, and the discovery made a sensation. We reached Paris before 8 o'clock. Travelling by the P.L.M. Railway later in the evening I had a fright each time the crude brakes worked bumpily on stopping at Melun, Bois le Roi, and Fontainebleau.

Graphic Art in Paris

For several years Bennett drew and painted regularly, and a few examples of his water-colours and sketches are owned by the Victoria and Albert Museum. The three-volume edition of the *Journal* has four sketches in the second volume, and the *Florentine Journal,* published in 1967, contains eighteen. It is not known when Bennett studied with Pierre Laprade (1875–1931), but presumably the date was 1909–10. The prize water-colour that he alludes to was used for the dustjacket of the American edition of *Sacred and Profane Love* (called there *The Book of Carlotta*), which George Doran issued in 1911.

The *Journal* of the years in France provides repeated testimony of Bennett's sense of his Englishness. Thus on 31 July 1904: "I had a lot of curious sensations on returning to England after an absence of 7 months – especially on wakening up in an English house – shaking off France, and readjusting my perspective of England and finding how fine England was and how I was full of sympathy for it, and all that sort of thing." Thus on 30 September 1909: "My first vague impression was here at last defined, of Paris. Namely the perversity and corruption of the faces, the numbers of women more or less chic also impressed me." Bennett gave up his French homes in 1911, and in 1913 he and Marguerite moved into Comarques, Thorpe-le-Soken, Essex.

The following piece was the concluding section of "My Reminiscences".

After an interval of a quarter of a century, I had resumed, by some caprice, my early practice in water-colour painting. One of my school-girlish productions hung framed in the drawing-room of a Parisian friend, whose taste was, at any rate in this instance, unduly influenced by his affections, but who had a large and intimate acquaintance among the most modern French artists – by which I mean among the school known in England as the Post Impressionists, the school which was guffawed at a dozen years ago in England, was treated with marked respect by *The Times* ten years ago, and which in a few years more will be worshipped in England as ignorantly as it was once condemned. I had a particular admiration for the water-colour of Pierre Laprade, a light of this school, and I told my friend I should like to meet my hero. Nothing easier! We met without delay at lunch. Before the lunch I had said to my friend: "On no account let him see my water-colour."

My friend answered: "I shall most assuredly show him your water-colour."

❖   ❖   ❖

I pretended to be desolated; but, naturally with the naive hopefulness of the rank amateur, I was secretly pleased. My hero was led to my water-colour, and gazed thereat with indifferent disapproval.

"Monsieur," he said to me, "you have three times too much cleverness, and your work is utterly without interest."

It is scarcely credible, but I felt flattered. I was enchanted that I had three times too much cleverness. M. Laprade and I grew friendly; I visited his studio. We discussed art.

"The only advice I can offer to you", he said, "is to wait until you are conscious of an emotion before an object, and then paint what you feel."

Shortly afterwards I happened to be conscious of an emotion before an object – namely, the courtyard of the old house in Paris where I was living. So I painted what I felt one December afternoon. I then invited M. Laprade to lunch, and left the watercolour lying about. He spied it quickly enough.

"*Mon Dieu!*" he cried, too amiably excited. "You've done it!

Oh, you've done it this time! *Très bien! Très bien!* Very interesting! Veritably interesting!"

(I should have kept this masterpiece as a sort of milestone in my swift career as a Post Impressionist, had not my American publisher caught sight of it and walked off with it, unintimidated by its post-impressionism. "I shall use this as a "jacket" [paper covering] for one of your books," he said. And he did. He had it reproduced in colours, and calmly placed it on the bookstalls of the United States. I learnt afterwards that it was considered by trade experts as among the best commercial "jackets" of its season. Such can be the fruits of an emotion!)

❖   ❖   ❖

My hero suggested that if I wished to take painting seriously I might attend the Post Impressionist Academy of which he was a professor. I was afraid; but, being ashamed of my timidity, I said I would go with the greatest pleasure. He took me. I entered the studio under his majestic aegis as his *protégé*. It was a fearful moment. I was ten times more nervous than I have ever been when called before the curtain of a theatre. I trembled, literally. It seemed absurd that I, a school-girlish amateur, should be there in that most modern of Parisian studios as a serious student of art. However, I had burnt my boats. I had to summon my manhood and begin a charcoal drawing of the model, a young Italian girl. I scarcely knew what I was doing. I glanced surreptitiously at the other students – about a dozen or so. The other students glanced surreptitiously at me. They were all young, extraordinarily young when compared with myself. I knew then that I was middle-aged. The studio was large and of irregular shape, and the stove was red-hot. Two young men in yellow smocks were painting, close together, and two other men sat behind, smoking, restlessly getting up and sitting down again. Silence. Dusk (3.50 p.m.). I looked about me. There were large photographs of modern masterpieces on the walls, a table with reviews on it, dumb-bells on the floor close to, a fiddle-case and a volume of Mozart on a shelf. At the second "rest" I persuaded myself that it was absurd to be discountenanced by a pack of boys. So I joined a group of them in the jauntiest manner I could assume and made artistic small-talk.

"Come and have a look at my drawing," I said, in a humorous tone. "Criticise it." (M. Laprade had disappeared.)

They came, politely. They gazed at the thing and said not a word.

"Of course, the head's too small," I remarked airily.

"In effect," said one of them gravely, "the head is rather small."

Nobody said anything else. The sitting was resumed.

❖   ❖   ❖

Going home M. Laprade advised me to paint a water-colour of the Tuileries gardens from the Pavilion des Arts Decoratifs. Also to go and examine carefully the Delacroix at St Sulpice, and then get a photograph of it, and do a water-colour interpretation of it from memory at home. We called at a colour-maker's to buy sketch-books, etc. His demeanour towards the respectful and somewhat intimidated students had been quite informal, or nearly so. He told me that when *he* first came to Paris, there would be a great crowd of students in a large atelier; a professor (of German aspect) would come in; all the students would stand up; and the professor would march about curtly from one canvas to the next, making such remarks as, "That leg is too short."

❖   ❖   ❖

It might be thought that after this baptism into a cult so acutely Parisian, I should have felt myself more than ever firmly rooted in the soil of France. But it was not so. For several years there had been gradually germinating in my mind the conviction that I should be compelled by some obscure instinct to return to England, where, unhappily, art is not cherished as in France. I had a most disturbing suspicion that I was losing touch with England, and that my (literary) work would soon begin to suffer accordingly. And one day I gave notice to my landlady, and then I began to get estimates for removing my furniture and books. And then I tried to sell to my landlady the fittings of the admirable bathroom which I had installed in her house, and she answered

153

me that she had no desire for a bathroom in her house, and would I take the fittings away? And then I unhooked my pictures and packed my books. And lastly, the removers came and turned what had been a home into a litter of dirty straw. And I saw the tail of the last van as it rounded the corner. And I gave up my keys so bright with use. And I definitely quitted the land where eating and love are understood, where art and learning are honoured, where women well dressed and without illusions are not rare, where thrift flourishes, where politeness is practised, and where politics are shameful and grotesque. I return merely as a visitor. I should probably have enjoyed myself more in France, only I prefer to live in England and regret France than to live in France and regret England. I think the permanent exile is a pathetic figure. I suppose I have a grim passion for England. But I know why France is the darling of nations.

Clay in the
Hands of the Potter

Bennett made use of the pottery industry in *Anna of the Five Towns*, but otherwise he gave little attention to it in the novels. The following essay appeared in the *Windsor Magazine* in December 1913, and in *Youth's Companion* in America two months earlier.

ꙮ   ꙮ   ꙮ

Although the world, when it takes any interest at all in the Five Towns, identifies the district with clay, I do not think that I have ever seen Five Towns children playing at being potters. At the period when local history begins, earthen vessels were being made in the Five Towns, and certainly there is an unbroken record of at least twelve hundred years of pottery manufacture down there; it is equally certain that I myself have the clay in my blood, for my grandfather had the reputation of unsurpassed skill as a "turner", and scores of my forbears must, like him, have earned a living by the actual handling of clay. Yet I never felt any curiosity concerning the great staple industry – surely one of the oldest of man's crafts – until I was twenty-nine or thirty, when I wanted some information about it for a novel. The fact is that half the people of the Five Towns have no knowledge of the industry, and are quite content in their ignorance. The industry goes on behind the long, many-windowed mysterious walls of innumerable manufactories, and the ignorant half pass up and down the façades of those buildings, and let the matter go at that. They see neither the raw clay, which is brought by sea and canals from afar off, nor the finished articles, which leave the works hidden in straw-stuffed crates. And if you want to buy a plate or a cup and saucer, there is positively no worse equipped place in the civilised world. This is, no doubt, human.

But when at last I did put myself to the trouble of visiting and comprehending a modern earthenware manufactory – it belonged to one of my uncles, and he was very proud of his new machinery – the gateway of romance was opened to me. I saw, as it were, in a sudden revelation, what a wonderful, ticklish, sensitive, capricious, baffling, unreasonable substance is clay. I could appreciate why its behaviour under handling had puzzled a whole province for a dozen centuries and more, and still puzzles.

In my uncle's manufactory some two hundred individuals spend their lives in trying to get the better of clay, with or without the aid of machinery. The machinery, in my opinion, despite my relative's pride in it, was not essentially very important; it only bullied the clay by physical force, or divided it into mathematically equal quantities, or shaped it into certain simple forms. The machinery was pretentious and blustering; it never helped in a real difficulty.

In an earthenware manufactory they have, after twelve centuries, thoroughly learnt one lesson, namely, that clay is a living thing, and therefore enigmatic. Indeed, it presents so many enigmas that the potters have had to divide their forces and attack the creature by instalments. A plate may appear to you to be a ridiculously simple article; and you think that if you had to make it, you would just dig up the right sort of clay, fashion it, and then burn it. But the right sort of clay does not naturally exist. The basis of every earthenware manufactory is a workshop where bearded and reverend men thoughtfully examine several different natural sorts of clay, and cause them to be mixed together by the brute force of machines, in the hope that the product will be white and serviceable. These men are grey – they have grown grey in the vain study of bits of their mother-earth, which still not seldom play them tricks – and they are the descendants of similar men.

And by their side you will see a youth or two, watching them and helping, and picking up notions of the exceeding "plaguiness" of clay. And the hair of these youths, too, will turn, and the clay will still be inventing new problems for them.

These men have naught to do with the shaping of clay. They would be capable of looking at a plate and saying: "What is this? I have never seen such a thing!" Their affair is only with clay in the shapeless mass.

Another set of men take up the attack when the time comes for persuading clay to assume definite forms. And these men and their boys and their women-helpers correspond better than the first group with your conventional idea of the potter. Their fingers really are manipulating a pale malleable substance which you would at once recognise as clay. Machinery helps them, but merely as a brainless servant. In many manufactures the man is the servant of the machine; it will probably never be so in pottery. The fingers of these men and boys are finer tools than any wood or metal could be. See the boy pull off a piece of clay from the big lump and roll it; watch his fingers – that boy's fingers might be twelve hundred years old in skill. Look away and then look back, and lo! what was a hunch of clay is a little plate, and there is no clay left over. The boy had pulled off precisely the right quantity of clay for a vessel of which the dimensions had to conform precisely to a pattern.

See the man gazing at the plate, caressing it with a healing touch, and pushing it aside. See the man near by making a mug with his fingers over a revolving table. The mug grows like a flower; the man seems to be drawing it upwards by magic out of the table. The table comes to a standstill – and there the mug is, perfect! See the minor workers carrying off these soft and fragile vessels with apparent casualness. If you or I touched one of them, the result would be ruin. These people, however, understand clay – as well as clay can be understood – in that particular stage of its career. Their sympathy with clay shaped but unfired is the slow result of all those centuries. But their sympathy goes no farther than that. The idiosyncrasies of clay under fire are beyond their ken.

And we come back to yet another set of students of clay, the men who imprison the clay – now in the form of vessels, but entirely useless as such – in a vast fiery inferno, the men who victimise clay, who change clay so effectually that it can by no chemical process ever be changed back again to its original state. These men are more mystically priest-like than the others. They often work at night. Once a job is begun, they never under any consideration leave it till it is finished. A single indiscretion, and thousands of pounds' worth of moulded clay may be rendered futile and valueless. And they themselves do not know what is going on in the inferno which they have created. They can only hope that the clay under the ordeal of fire is not behaving too obstreperously, for it is obvious that they may not enter their own inferno to see how affairs are moving. They have to guess. They are very good guessers. They have been guessing since before the Norman Conquest of England. But a guess remains a guess. And when they let the fire die down, their pessimism or their optimism asserts itself, and during the cooling period torments or enheartens them. The cooling period is long – nearly a couple of days – and even then the ovens are so hot that you or I could not enter them without fainting. But the potter, stripped to the waist, enters nonchalantly the ghostly interior, lined and piled with pale martyred vessels, and carries them out in parcels, and at last, in the light of day, the experts can regard the clay and decide whether it has beaten them again. It always does beat them to a certain extent. What is this yellow stain on this tea-pot? Nobody can tell. A caprice of the clay, the clay's freakish protest against fire. Sometimes a whole ovenful of stuff is damaged, sometimes only a small percentage; but never, never does the entire consignment of clay behave as it was expected to behave and as it ought to behave.

And even now your simple, easy-looking plate is far from achieved. It looks rather more like a whitewashed dog-biscuit than a plate. It generally has to be decorated – at any rate, it has to be glazed – and it has to go through the ordeal of fire at least once more – perhaps twice more. And each further process is a new opportunity for the clay to prove its intractableness and its unforeseeableness. And each further process is presided over by lifelong students of just that particular part of the clay's evolution. Even the packer, sitting among straw and wrapping up each piece separately and protecting the clay from itself, has to know quite a lot about the wilfulness of earthenware when subjected to certain strains. Earthenware will often maintain itself intact in a railroad smash, only to shatter in the delicate touch of a general servant aged nineteen. Have you not heard her say: "Please'm, the handle came off in my hand." To the very last, clay is incalculable.

Decoration plays a more and more important part in the staple industry of the Five Towns. Housewives want gayer and more gilded crockery, and they also want to pay less for it. Hence the invention of cheaper methods of more gorgeous decoration. Now, clay is not so restive under decoration as might be imagined. But the antics played by fire on the colour-substances cause difficulties which rival the original difficulties due to the natural perverseness of the clay itself. And all this part of the manufacture is less interesting to the workman than the handling of the clay. It is an affair of the mechanical transfer of patterns designed elsewhere, and the mechanical application of pigments for which distant and unknown chemists are alone responsible. Nevertheless, the simpler and better forms of decoration remain, and with them the unspoilt human interest that is inseparable from them. For instance, round the edge of that plate there may be a couple of rings of colour, one broad and the other narrow. In the Five Towns this is called "band-and-line" decoration. It seems, on the plate, to be too miraculously perfect for human accomplishment. And yet it was done by hand, and by a young woman's hand, and will probably always be so done.

In the manufactories, the painting-shops, where the band-and-line goes forward, are the quietest and, as a rule, the cleanest of all the shops – often very noticeably more spick-and-span than the den in which the head of the enterprise conducts his wholesale schemes. For these painting-shops are under the dominion of young women who have an enormous idea of themselves as factors in the universe. You may see them, if you arise soon enough, on the early tram-cars and trains, or walking primly down the streets. They are very neat. They wear gloves – the supreme insignia of rank in these worlds within the world. Nay, I have seen them wearing kid gloves. They carry a small covered wicker-basket, which basket contains their dinner. They arrive at the "pot-bank" – as an earthenware manufactory is called in the Five Towns – and, lifting their skirts over the impurities that disfigure most parts of it, they reach their own sacred fastness, and put away their street things and don a large white apron – and when I say white I mean white. They then attend to their brushes and their colours, and they sit down, each of them, to a tiny revolving table, with a pile of plates or saucers or cups or mugs at one hand.

See them take a vessel and with one unerring gesture plant it exactly in the centre of the table. See them take a broad brush and hold it firmly and gently against the edge of the now spinning vessel. The "band" is made; it is made in a second! A thinner brush, and with equal precision the line is made. And that vessel is pushed off the table, and another pushed on. And then another, and then another. Dozens! Scores! Hundreds! And then a bell rings, or a hooter hoots, for one o'clock. And the young woman rises, goes elsewhere, primly eats her dinner, perhaps goes for a little walk. And when the next bell rings, or the next hooter hoots, she sits down again, and the table begins to revolve again. More dozens! More scores! More hundreds! At six o'clock she departs, gloved and hatted and mantled, and primly takes her tram-car or train, or perhaps walks home.

The next morning she starts afresh on exactly the same task. For you must remember that there are in existence millions upon millions of vessels decorated with band-and-line, and that they have all of them been painted separately by young women seated at revolving tables. It is a wondrous and a dreadful thought, but it is part of the singular romance of clay. The skill for the task is soon learnt. The task is monotonous in the highest degree. It is endless. You might suppose that its monotony and its endlessness would drive these young women into some form of lunacy or melancholia. But no! The vocation merely endows them with a sort of benignant placidity. Their faces are like no other faces, their movements like no other movements. Such intellect as they have may not be highly developed, but they possess qualities of calm, of patience, even of mild spiritual dignity which are – well, nun-like! They are among the most curious products of industrialism, and among the most curious by-products of the Odyssey of clay.

No person of imagination who has taken the trouble to follow with intelligence the Odyssey of clay, from its stratum in the earth to its apotheosis on the domestic table, can pick up a simple plate without a certain emotion. The clay of it is indeed dead, but what adventures led up to its fiery demise, and what human associations are imbedded in its everlasting rigidity! Strange, that Five Towns children do not play at being potters!

The Greatest Moment

The First World War came when Bennett was at the height of his reputation. He saw the war as the defence of civilisation, represented mainly by England and France, and he gave a great deal of time and energy to it. He became military representative on the Thorpe Division Emergency Committee, he served on a number of war committees concerned with the arts and with charities, he visited the Western Front and wrote a few articles of propaganda for the Government, and in 1918 he entered the Ministry of Information under Lord Beaverbrook. Beaverbrook offered him the post after reading *The Pretty Lady* (1918), whose heroine is a French cocotte. The job had to do with propaganda in France, and Beaverbrook thought that the novel displayed unusual understanding of the French. Except for the articles, all of this work was unpaid. Also unpaid were his "Observations" for the *New Statesman,* an anonymous column that appeared weekly during the last two years of the war. Most of the paid journalism during the war went to the *Daily News.* The articles there concerned the conduct of the war, and many of them were outspoken attacks on the Government.

Despite all of his war work, Bennett wrote two and a half novels and two plays during the war. *These Twain,* the last of the *Clayhanger* trilogy, published in 1916, was widely reviewed as his greatest achievement, and a few critics thought that *The Pretty Lady* was still better. Nevertheless he emerged from the war with a diminished reputation. Thereafter he was the famous novelist rather more than the greatest novelist.

The Greatest Moment

The following article appeared in the *Sunday Express* on 28 June 1925. It was reprinted in *Things That Have Interested Me, Third Series* in 1926.

⋙ ⋙ ⋙

Of course there are sensational moments in life particulars of which only a very communicative man will communicate to the world. Apart from such moments, I cannot recall that either before the war or after the war I experienced any thrills worth mentioning. But during the war a few thrills came my way.

As representative of the War Office, I had charge of the civil organisation for moving the entire population in case of need out of a certain area where the War Office believed the Germans would land – if they did land. I was talking to a considerable officer one night when he said to me gloomily:

"Why don't our aeroplanes destroy Essen? I will tell you. Because Asquith has shares in Krupps, and won't allow it."

It thrilled me to think how easily we should win the war under the direction of such master-minds as this one.

I had another and a different thrill when I was summoned by a Cabinet minister to a meeting of distinguished authors who were to help in putting Britain's case persuasively before the whole world – and especially America. I there learnt that very distinguished authors had been patriotically sending gratis articles to America and having them refused by very distinguished American editors. I thought that this difficulty might be overcome. I wrote an article stating the British case, and said:

"The price of this stuff is £300."

It was at once bought and printed. I wrote more and lengthier stuff, about our armies, and said:

"The price of this stuff is £1,800."

It was at once bought and printed. The editors were pleased. The British Government was pleased. And so was I. A great moment for the last-named!

❖ ❖ ❖

In the last year of the war I was summoned to the Ministry of Information and asked to sit in it and take charge of all British propaganda for France. The Minister told me that I understood the psychology of the French. I did not deny it. He also said:

"Whatever you do, I will back you."

He did.

I had always had a passion for organisation. I now gratified the passion. Next to running a great hotel, this business seemed to me to be the most sensational that any human being could indulge in. I could contradict and withstand ambassadors, and did.

But soon afterwards I had a fright, the most terrible of my life. I was told:

"The Minister is very ill, and will resign. No new Minister is to be appointed at present, but you will be put in charge of the Ministry, with supreme responsibility."

Imagine a wayward novelist, with no experience of bureaucratic methods, having dominion over hundreds of exalted persons, including bank directors, railway directors, historians, K.C.'s, heads of trusts, poets, and generals! You cannot. At least I could not. I told a Minister that I could not sleep for responsibility. He said:

"You will get used to it."

The strange thing is that I did.

Great and awful days! What tales I could tell of rival Ministries fighting one another quite as tenaciously as the Allied armies fought the German armies – and with far more bitterness. A friend of mine in the War Office told me that an order had been issued forbidding any member of his section, under any pretext whatever, to enter my Ministry.

Still, when I visited the War Office, even the mightiest swells had to see me. Which was something.

I had a few Generals of my own. I remember the first time I rang the bell and said to one of my secretaries:

"Ask General X if he will be good enough to come and see me at once."

And General X came and was received in audience. A great moment for a novelist! But if you think that it was the greatest of all, you are mistaken. My Generals, I ought to say, were charming and unbureaucratic men, and I had no sort of grievance against them. Nevertheless they were generals, and in summoning them I felt that I was doing something to redress the balance on behalf of all privates, and all officers from Colonels downwards, in all the British armies.

❖   ❖   ❖

The greatest moment of all, the moment when I knew that my life had touched its climax, was in November 1918, when my principal secretary came into my room and said:

"Fellows at the War Office are continually ringing me up to know whether the Armistice has been signed."

"Don't tell them," said I. (Not that we knew.)

Such was the co-ordination of Ministries in the war that I got my first news of the Armistice from a newsboy in Regent Street at 10.45 a.m. on 11th November. Everybody knew at eleven o'clock. I returned to my Ministry, the staff of which was highly excited and even hysterical, particularly the women. I affected nonchalance, and urged the women to remain calm. But perhaps this moment was the supremely great one for me, after all. I was free.

165

My Religious Experience

In the *Journal* on 15 October 1896 Bennett wrote:
"Essential characteristic of the really great novelist:
a Christ-like, all-embracing compassion." This was
an abiding belief, and it was also a belief about the
really great man. Whether Bennett himself was really
great as novelist or man was a matter of strong
opinion among friends and enemies. Certainly he was
notorious, and the publication of the following essay
began on the front page of the *Evening Standard* on 14
October 1925, and was announced by a headline
across the page. The essay appeared in the *Century
Magazine* in America in March 1926, and was reprinted
in *Things That Have Interested Me, Third Series*.

A month before the essay appeared in the *Standard*
Bennett published an article entitled "What I
Believe" in the *Daily Express*. That article was the
first of a series by famous people on their religious
beliefs, and it evoked considerable anger and some
praise among religious leaders. The Bishop of
Liverpool was one of those who approved, and two
years later he invited Bennett to write a small book on
religion for his "Affirmation" series. *The Religious
Interregnum* (1929) was the result. It expressed belief
that a religion of kindliness would succeed dogmatic
Christianity.

In my native town there were four principal churches of the Church of England and five principal chapels of Nonconformity. We Nonconformists had a double attitude towards the churches. Socially we admired and envied them. So much so that we often preferred to go to them for the religious ceremony of marriage, whereas we might have been just as securely married elsewhere. Religiously we despised Church of Englanders. They were not in our eyes so ineffably wicked or inexcusably misguided as Roman Catholics; but they were pretty far gone in error, wilful or stupid. Indeed, it was impossible to trust certain Nonconformist preachers, and especially lay preachers, without being convinced that all Church of Englanders were on the sure way to everlasting damnation.

For Nonconformists of whatever sect were generally agreed on this: that to keep out of hell it was absolutely necessary to be "converted". Good morals, good works, were futile without conversion. It was no use being born in the belief that Christ died on the cross to save sinners; you had to be "born again", you had suddenly to see a mystic light, under the influence of which you believed with a new and immeasurably intenser belief. Church of Englanders contemned this experience as being allied to hysteria. Nonconformists pitied them for their blindness.

The double attitude of Nonconformity towards the Established Church puzzled, and offended, such unsubtle minds as my own. Further, considering that comparatively few persons were converted, it followed that the vast majority of the citizens were damned. And whenever as a child I thought about the matter at all I smiled malevolently to think that at least 90 per cent of the wayfarers on pavements and in tram-cars would in due course join me in Hades, in spite of the fact that all of them had some religion. For in the seventies and eighties of the last century there were almost no "atheists" in our town. And if anybody did by chance ostentatiously deny the God of the Bible, sure enough he – I say "he" because female atheists were utterly unknown – he would one day, and soon rather than late, get himself converted in a manner equally ostentatious.

I will not say that I flouted the dogma of the Wesleyan Methodist sect. I suppose that I passively accepted it. But my acceptance of it had no emotional quality. The notion of being converted was very repugnant to me. I preferred damnation to conversion, as being less humiliating. The arguments in favour of the dogma did not make much appeal to me; nor was I impressed by the mentality of the individuals who marshalled those arguments before my attention. My counter-arguments (brought forward only in strictly private boy-to-boy debates) were painfully crude but rather effective. As for example: "If God is omniscient He knows whether I am going to heaven or hell. If He knows, the question is already decided. If it is already decided, what does it matter what I do?" Although the answer to this argument is quite simple and plausible, nobody ever suggested it to me. True, I did not dare to submit the point to the mighty.

❖   ❖   ❖

Nothing happened in my childhood to foster in me any religious faith. And there were many things calculated to destroy faith. One of these was the fact that some of the pillars of the chapel had a rather dubious reputation for commercial integrity. Dishonest myself, and unsaved, I was cruelly uncompromising in my verdicts on the conduct of the saved. But one thing that most damaged in me the chances of a secure religious belief was the religious misbehaviour of my father. So far as I can remember I never had any religious instruction at home. My father compelled us to go to chapel and Sunday school, but for many years he did not go to Sunday school himself, and he very seldom went to chapel. On the rare occasions when he did decide to go to evening chapel the awed word ran round the house: "Pa is going to chapel." And it was as though chapel ought to be grateful for his condescension.

Such a state of affairs was bound to give unreality to all professions of religious faith. We children felt that religious observance was imposed upon us, not for religious but for disciplinary reasons. And this suspicion, or certainty, made Sunday all the more odious to us. Sunday was the worst day of the week, anticipated with horror, and finished with an exquisite relief. Two attendances at Sunday school and two religious services in a day! About six hours in durance, while my father either lay in bed or read magazines in the bow window! It was inevitable that religion should come to be unalterably connected in my mind with the ideas of boredom, injustice, and insincerity.

❖   ❖   ❖

And sometimes the offence was outrageous. As when a minister had the monstrous and callous effrontery to institute a Bible class for boys on the Saturday half-holiday. The resentment which I felt at this innovation, and at my father's upholding of it, burns in my mind to-day. It was surpassed only by my resentment against a sudden capricious paternal command that we children should say our prayers at our mother's knee. There was, for me, something revolting in the sentimentality, the story-bookishness, of this injunction! Anyhow we loathed the act, which filled us with shame. Nobody could possibly in the history of the world have been in a mood more fatal to prayer than I was in the moments when I obeyed the command. I used to say bitterly to myself: "He likes to see us doing it." This did not, however, affect my general attitude towards prayer. Neither before nor since did I ever say a prayer with the slightest hope of it being answered.

When at the age of twenty-one I left home for London, one of the leading thoughts in my head was that I should be free of chapels and Sunday schools, and the desolation of Sabbaths. Such was the main result of my father's education of me in ceremonial religion, acting on my mocking and sceptical temperament. I had no religious beliefs and I was profoundly inimical to all manifestations of religion. In various other ways my father's influence on me was admirable, and I owe a great deal to it. I regret that I should have to lay stress on that part of his training in which he failed.

❖   ❖   ❖

When I came to London and was free to direct my own existence according to my own ideas, I did, partly in a spirit of discovery and partly from habit, visit a few chapels and churches, but I very soon became indifferent to all the forms and rites of dogmatic religion; and religion, in the accepted sense of the word, ceased

169

entirely to enter into my life. This was not the result of mental sloth. My conscience was not in the least disturbed. I did not feel that I was leaving undone things that I ought to do. I shared of course the widespread objection to dying, but I had no qualms about the unpleasant possibilities of a life beyond the grave for a man who was failing to perform an act of belief. Heaven and hell meant nothing to me. The wrath of God meant nothing to me. No variety of dogma could hold my attention. I was not actively concerned about the divine purpose or the nature of God.

One cause of my indifference was the cautious, agnostic, and self-sufficient bent of my mind. But the main cause of it undoubtedly lay in a profound conviction that the riddle of the universe was insoluble by human reason and that therefore the wise course for me was to leave it alone. I was told that religion was beyond reason. Nevertheless, all dogmatists were continually appealing to my reason – as indeed all dogmatists are bound to do. In any case, they appealed quite in vain. My difficulty was, and is, absolutely fundamental.

My reason was incapable of conceiving the act of creation. Others may be able to conceive an act of creation. I cannot. I can conceive something being made out of something else. I can conceive men developing from the amoeba. But I cannot conceive something being made out of nothing. Suppose that I have the power of a divine creator. I stretch out my hand with open palm, in nothingness. I exercise the power to create, and lo! something is lying in the palm of my hand that was not there before! Well, I can suppose it, but I cannot conceive it as actually happening. I cannot see how it could happen. My mind has not the capacity for this feat. (Similarly with the conception of destruction.)

Hence I am forced to conclude that the universe, in some material form or other, was always in existence. But the word "always" involves infinity, and I cannot conceive infinity – either of time or anything else. I can carry my imagination backward through countless aeons and still further and further backward, but not infinitely backward, so that at last I have to say: "Everything must have had a beginning." Which is equivalent to saying: "At some time something must have been created – or made out of nothing." And I am thrown down again into my original difficulty. I see plainly that there must be some Life-Force – call it

God; but my mind has not the power even to conceive the nature of God at all.

◇   ◇   ◇

I have never been able to overcome this incapacity of mine. It has long since ceased to worry me. A religious need must presuppose a God, and it must be based in convictions about the nature of God. I marvel at the minds of unquestionably great men who have come to definite decisions as to what God is, what He thinks, how He acts. The daring of the doctrine of the Trinity staggers me. The subtlety of the altercations connected with, for example, the Athanasian and the Nicene creeds makes me dizzy. But I can feel no practical interest in these exercises of finite reason upon the infinite. I am, quite honestly and without any false modesty, too humble for them.

We all of us have to divide phenomena into the knowable and the unknowable. Dogmatists of every creed apparently know things which by me are unknowable. What can I do to remedy the imperfection of my mind? I should not object to having a religious creed. I should rather like to have one. A genuine creed must be a very convenient and comfortable thing. But how can I get it? I am told that I ought to try to believe. But why should I *try* to believe? Trying to believe, for me, means bullying or forcing or dethroning my reason; it means pretending that my mind can accomplish what I am convinced that it is incapable of accomplishing. I cannot do this, and I have no desire to attempt it. I am speaking only for myself; nevertheless I am well acquainted with many people who are in precisely my case.

◇   ◇   ◇

I have often read, and sometimes I have been told by word of mouth, that it is impossible for a normal man to gaze upon certain of this world's spectacles without being intimately convinced of the existence and the goodness of a Creator, and that therefore such spectacles alone must give a man religious faith – whether in his pride he acknowledges it or not. I agree that spectacles like a starlit night, a fine sunset (but more especially a fine sunrise), or a venerable cathedral full of stained glass, architectural style, incense, music, and the tradition of centuries of worship – I agree that these and kindred spectacles do arouse in my mind emotions which are vaguely uplifting, ennobling, and lovely. I say further that these emotions urge me, vaguely and temporarily, towards daily well-doing. But I do not agree that such spectacles help me in the slightest degree to form ideas about God clear and concrete enough to serve as a basis for religious belief. They do not even persuade me that there is any such being as a God existing entirely separate from myself. What they produce in me is awe, wonder, moral and artistic stimulation, and a grateful, contemplative pleasure in the simple fact that I am alive.

Moreover, I obtain just such emotions from all the phenomena of the universe. I cannot walk along a common street, while attentively examining in it all the astonishing and curious minute evidences of man's unconquerable determination to fulfil himself, without being imbued with a deep sense of the majesty and beauty of the whole inexplicable affair. The older I grow the more keenly I delight in the marvel of life. My reason stands apart, suspending its judgment indefinitely . . . Nor does this suspension of judgment incommode me the least in the world. I do not long to look up to anything in sure faith. I can exist quite well without. I should not mind having something exterior to myself to cling to, to lean upon, to appeal to for help in moments of difficulty; but I can manage unaided. I rather exult in the necessity of carrying on without help. I do not feel dwarfed nor humbled by the vastness and sublimity of my environment, for I am rooted in the private assurance that there is nothing more wondrous, or possessing greater ultimate potentialities, than the individual man.

❖   ❖   ❖

Many years ago I had a dream, and in the dream I stood by my own dead body and saw the pennies upon my eyes. I cannot remember at this distance of time what the rest of the dream was, but it had to do with the adventures of the soul after death. This dream, while it convinced me of nothing and gave me no faith in a future life, made a considerable impression upon me as an artist, and I expanded the idea and the mood into a novel, which I called

The Glimpse, the glimpse being of what lies beyond death. For the purpose of the novel I read a little in Oriental theology and philosophy, and out of that and out of such notions as I had previously met with I constructed a theory of the future and put it into a more or less realistic form.

I was amazed, almost frightened, by the quantity and the quality of the letters which reached me from various parts of the world, about the book (which nevertheless never had any sensational sale). The letters were not brilliant nor in any way striking, except in this: they revealed an intense and passionate curiosity about the future life. I saw that for very many people the nature of the future life was the question of all questions – a problem continually, perhaps continuously, at the back of their minds. The letters were such as one was obliged, in mere decency, to reply to – so poignant were they, so appealing. (Later, these letters began to affect my nerves, and I destroyed the bulk of them, and felt lightened of a load of human disquietude.)

At first I answered simply that the supernatural parts of my novel were inventions of mine or the result of appropriations from other speculators, that I had originally no interest in the problem other than an artistic interest, and that the book being finished and published I had no genuine interest in the problem at all and must therefore decline to join any of their societies for supernatural study or even to enter into arguments by correspondence. These earlier letters hurt or offended the recipients, and I perceived that I had not been tender enough towards the deepest feelings of my correspondents. Henceforward I modified the curt, uncompromising tone of my replies. So far as my memory goes there was not a correspondent who did not tremendously desire to believe in the immortality of the soul, and there were few who had failed to believe in it. (Not many of them were orthodox Christians.)

❖   ❖   ❖

I saw then, as in a revelation, how different was the bent of my mind from that of the minds of all my unknown correspondents. As regards the theory set forth in my novel, I had naturally made it as plausible as I could to my own reason. But I never had the slightest belief in it, nor instinctive tendency to believe in it, nor wish to believe in it. I could discover no proof or presumption satisfactory to myself, that my soul had or had not existed before earthly birth, or that it would or would not survive after earthly death. Mathematical difficulties alone (as to the numbers of souls existing at any given moment) might well, I thought, render all the rival theories of immortality equally untenable.

Further, I could not even conceive my soul save in terms of matter.

And to-day I remain in the same unspeculative mood. I do not speculate, because I cannot discern any possibility of a positive result to my speculations. But my state is not therefore gloomy or hopeless or listless. Not a bit. For whether my soul has existed from everlasting or was born at the birth of my body, and whether my soul will cease with my body or continue in being for ever, I have in any case the certain assurance that it exists now and that my duty is to develop it in the best way according to my lights. If it survives as an entity, well and good – my efforts toward the improvement of it cannot be lost. If it does not survive as an entity, and at death is separated into its original particles, still well and good – my efforts must have had their effect on the undying particles. It is scientifically incredible that any effort should not have its due consequence – and an eternal consequence. And so it comes to pass that in living this present life without worrying myself about any other life, I can find scope for all my longings – and yet live in eternity too. Unhesitatingly I dismiss the singular notion that any other life can be more "divine" in essence than this present life.

❖   ❖   ❖

Of course, after all, I have a dogma. Nor have I yet talked intimately with any man who had not. I doubt if life would be possible without one. If it is convenient to call my dogma my religion, let my dogma be so called. The theory of evolution has been scientifically proved to the satisfaction of the great majority of intelligent and thinking persons. We see illustrations of evolution everywhere and all the time. Evolution is the development of organisms in themselves and in their relations to other organisms. Now my dogma is that, in its broadest aspect, the movement of evolution is from something worse to something better. It is that human nature, with all its ups and downs, does improve – however slowly.

This assertion rests on no scientific basis. Its truth cannot be demonstrated. Indeed, many weighty and honest minds refuse to accept it, and I cannot by any process of rational argument show that they are wrong. Far from that, I am bound to admit that comparisons between present civilisation and past, between present philosophy and past, seem often to favour the past rather than the present. Nevertheless, I feel intensely that we are travelling from imperfection to perfection, and that here is the sole immediate answer to the enigma of the universe. If I did not feel this, if the consciousness of it did not permeate the whole of my existence, then I should become indifferent to life and would just as soon be dead, in the completest final sense, for ever and ever.

Fortified by my dogma, I find in life a divine savour that never satisfies, and I live eagerly.

The famous theory about the principle of evil warring against the principle of good has no significance for me. To me evil is a purely negative conception. Evil is the lack, or the insufficiency, of good. There is no devil; there is only a growing good. Not that I have any expectation of perfection being attained, either in this life or in any future life, either by myself or by any other component parts of the universe. I strive after perfection. But I do not want actually to get it. Perfection is static. It destroys every motive for endeavour, and therefore renders the universe meaningless and futile – for me. Salvation – no! Salvation would be death. If I am to live I must not be saved; I must never be sure of salvation. Danger, struggle, conflict – these things alone constitute life, and more than aught else it is life that I desire.

◆　　◆　　◆

I have spoken of self-sufficiency, and thereby have perhaps exposed myself to the charge of spiritual pride – an attribute which I detest almost as much as I detest anything. But I do not think that a refusal, or an inability, to trust blindly in that which I am incapable of comprehending, can properly be denounced as spiritual pride. Nor do I think, either, that to count myself as actually part of the divine force which makes my heart beat can be so treated. For as a fact I myself am just as incomprehensible and marvellous as anything exterior to me in the universe. I cannot fathom God, and I cannot fathom myself.

Again, my self-sufficiency is directed solely towards an unknown supposed Creator alleged to be exterior to myself – if such there be. It certainly does not extend to my fellow-men. For in the first place, I regard them all as equally divine with myself in their essence. And in the second place, I feel constantly the need of their companionship and support.

In a book so full of terrible pictures of the deity as the Bible, the phrase "God is love" may appear strange, even out of place. Nevertheless, this phrase, for me, contains all divine wisdom and is the key to the conduct of life. If we are all part of God, we must all love. Love means charity, humility, forgiveness, self-forgetfulness, kindliness. To think kind thoughts of others, and never to think unkind thoughts, is, for me, the summit of righteousness, the secret of happiness, and the only gateway to any success worth calling success. The oftener I read the Sermon on the Mount the more deeply am I convinced that here is the final practical wisdom. I disagree with the view that Christ's moral teaching will not stand the test of modern conditions. I think it will. But immense courage is needed to follow it, and exceedingly few of us have the necessary courage. It may be, and ought rightly to be, a counsel of perfection. Yet what other counsels should we seek?

In no field of human thought has the teaching of Christ been more disastrously ignored than in theology. Millions of people have killed and been killed, tortured and been tortured, ostracised and been ostracised, because of differences about the proper attitude towards the Unknowable. Dogma may be necessary to humanity, but it has been the occasion of nearly every sin. The original reason for all this fury and pride was probably the violence and sincerity of the belief in the supreme, vital importance of particular dogmas.

To-day the face of things is changed. The fury has abated, the pride is a little bowed down. Dogma has become less dogmatic. And partly on this account, and partly owing to an increase of reasonableness we no longer murder, or curse to everlasting hell, those who do not think as we do in the domain of theological speculation. I for one would not dream of going forth with a hatchet to destroy anybody who declined to subscribe to my dogma that the movement of evolution is from something worse to something better. And most people are now like me in respect to their dogmas. We have in some degree actually educated ourselves to perceive that there never was a dogma which did not contain some hint of the truth, and that there never will be one which contains the whole truth! This new breadth of mind is in itself an advance towards the religion of kindliness. For many years I was full of hatred, resentment, and scorn for the fierce upholders of the cult which clouded my youth. Now I am humbler. Those religionists had terrific ideals, even though kindliness in thought and broad tolerance were not among them. And if they arrogated to themselves the authority of God they were unconsciously demonstrating the divinity of man.

Would I Live My Life Again?

The following article appeared in the *Sunday Express* on 13 March 1929. It was the first in a series of responses by famous people to the question posed by the title.

ﻌﻌ   ﻌﻌ   ﻌﻌ

Before answering the question: Would I, if I had the chance, live my life over again? I should ask several other questions: Do you mean the same life? And do you mean that I should be aware, during my second life, that I had adorned or disfigured the earth on a previous occasion? Or do you mean that I should be totally unaware that this was my second effort in the great enterprise?

If you mean that I should live the same life with full cognisance of the past, I reply that not on any account would I live the same or a similar life again, because I should all the time know what was going to happen, and in my opinion nothing can be more awful, more nerve-racking, more tedious than insight into the future.

If you intend me to live the same life without knowledge of the past, my reply is that I wouldn't absolutely object, for I have had an exciting and a romantic existence full of interest, though with many bad quarters of an hour in it. At the same time I do not see much point in living my life over again unless I knew that I was I, and not nobody in particular.

If you mean that, without conscious knowledge of my earlier past, I should still unconsciously possess the experience then acquired, I reply that the adventure would be unnatural and absurd. Unnatural because a human being cannot have the energetic curiosity of youth and the wisdom of age simultaneously. Absurd because either I should ignore the past experience, or, acting upon it in tender years, I should appear ridiculous both to myself and my fellow-creatures.

Further, the old experience would anyhow probably be worse than useless in the new conditions in which I should find myself. A young man who in the 1940's behaved as young men behaved in the 1880's would stand a fair chance of being lynched or at best of being ostracised by society. No! On the whole the notion of a second earthly life does not strongly attract me.

To come to the present life and its problems, there is the great question regarding happiness: Ought we to go out for happiness as being the most important human need? I must ask: What do you mean by happiness? Do you mean pleasure, amusement, excitement? Or do you mean something less strenuous, such as quiet content?

If you mean the former, let me point to the people who, being rich, give their whole lives to the search for happiness, seeking it in travel, luxury, change and diversion – otherwise "having a good time". Are they, in any sense of the word, happy? The answer is no. On the contrary they are generally bored, discontented, selfish, and frustrated.

This fact is notorious; the victims realise the fact, but their moral stamina is so enfeebled by their mode of life that they lack the strength of mind to profit by their knowledge. They sink from bad to worse. Gloomy and apprehensive themselves, beneath a factitious gaiety, they spread a miserable pessimism around them. The conclusion is that, whatever happiness may be, these earnest and feverish seekers after it never discover it. Yet many of them have brains!

You may say that money is a handicap and will not buy anything worth buying. I disagree. The general instinct of mankind to obtain money is a sound instinct. Money is certainly not a handicap. Money will buy nearly everything – except a clear conscience and a cheerful temperament. It will buy comfort. It will buy

quite a lot of health. If it is used with skill it will buy love, genuine love. Crowds of rich men have been deeply and lastingly
loved by gifted and beautiful women who would never have
looked twice at them had they been poor men. Which, when you
think it over, is very natural.

Money will even buy fame – at a price. (So will murder). Large
numbers of people are convinced that fame – good fame – is the
most enviable thing in the world. It assuredly is not.

The advantages of fame are that it endows the possessor with a
certain perhaps justifiable self-complacency (a very doubtful
advantage), and that it inspires his friends and acquaintances, and
especially his tradesmen, to put themselves out of the way in
order to be of service to him. A famous man always enjoys the
"most-favoured-nation" clause in the social treaty. (This advantage is real!)

One of the disadvantages of fame is that it also inspires envy
and malice. A second disadvantage is that it lays upon the holder
the curse of self-consciousness in public. Let him enter any
public place – restaurant, theatre, hall – and he will see individuals
whispering to one another, and he well knows that they are saying: "Look! That's the famous X!" Of course the whisperers are
guilty of bad manners, but they will do it. Try as he may, the
famous X will lose his naturalness of demeanour. Some famous
X's revel in the disturbing publicity. Others detest it. But in
either case it cannot be said to help to create a permanent state
of happiness of any sort.

On the whole I would say that fame helps slightly more towards happiness than towards unhappiness. As a means towards
felicity I would rank it about equal with money. And about equal
with good health. And about equal with a clear conscience. And
far lower than a steady reciprocated affection for a person of the
opposite sex. And far higher than passionate love. I shall be con-
tradicted. But I am a realist, not a sentimentalist.

It is indisputable that many rich men, many famous men, many
healthy men, many men with clear consciences, and many men in
love and loved, are unhappy. And it is indisputable that many
poor men, many obscure men, many ill men, many men with
clouded consciences, many men neither loving nor loved, are not
unhappy. Hence, we have not so far hit upon a trustworthy path

to happiness – even defining happiness as a state of mild content, or a state of not being positively unhappy. And the reason is, in my opinion, that happiness must not be regarded as a goal.

If I have learnt anything from life, this is what I have learnt: The man who makes his chief objective the attainment of happiness is bound to fail in his endeavour and to die disillusioned.

Happiness is a by-product – and there is not a vast deal of it anyway. It is a by-product of self-fulfilment, which is the most important thing in the world, and which should be the goal of every sensible person.

The worst fate that can befall is to reach old age, or to die, with the conviction that you have not tried your best to do what your most powerful instinct urged you to do, that your energies have been misdirected or idle, in short, you have been stultified. A man stultified is an unhappy man. A man who has honestly striven to fulfil himself may not be wildly happy: he may meet with terrible misfortunes; but beneath every dissatisfaction there will be a constant, stronger, permeating satisfaction. This satisfaction comes as near to happiness as any enduring sensation can.

Of course, there are people who have no powerful instinct. Ask them at the outset of their careers what they want to do with themselves, and they answer that they are aware of no preferences, and do not mind what they do. In practice they take up the first job that comes to hand, and usually they are content. Yet the majority of us are inclined to despise them in their tepid contentedness. Which shows that we do not in our hearts consider contentedness to be the supreme ideal.

Withal, self-fulfilment does not imply that the major instinct is to be favoured at the expense of all the other instincts which are included in the composition of the self. A man may give so much licence to his major instinct that it finishes by killing him. Such a man has not fulfilled himself; he has merely made a tragic fool of himself.

The major instinct must govern, but only as a constitutional monarch. A man's body, his pocket, his private and intimate relationships, even his conscience, may have to suffer under the rule of the major instinct; but if they, or some of them, are allowed to suffer too much, self-fulfilment is scotched. The man becomes a monster, as Napoleon, for example, became a monster, or any paltry miser in a back street.

Finally, there are two aids to happiness more effective than health and wealth and fame, immensely more effective than sex-love, and, I should say, somewhat more effective than an unspotted conscience (if such a phenomenon as an unspotted conscience indeed exists).

The first is a cheerful temperament, which is a gift from heaven. It cannot be created by taking thought, but it can be cultivated, enhanced, and magnified by taking thought – hourly thought.

The second is kindliness of heart, which is the best of all tonics for a temperament inclined towards the dismal. A cheerful temperament may be, and often is, the expression of a heart of flint but rarely, if ever, is kindliness of heart allied to a gloomy temperament. Contentedness must have its root in self-fulfilment, but the precious plant will blossom more beautifully in an atmosphere of kindliness. Kindliness, not merely in action, but in thought and in tone, is a sovereign antidote to melancholy and discouragement. Self-fulfilment can never be complete unless it is tempered by self-forgetfulness and self-sacrifice.

This axiom is not sentimentalism; it is realism. And the self-centred, ambitious individuals who ignore it or ruthlessly flout it are swollen blockheads. And you can behold them in all their glory and success of achievement, and still say: "Blockheads!" Say it kindly, though. They know no better.